# Blood&Bone

# Blood&Bone

POEMS BY PHYSICIANS

*Edited by* Angela Belli & Jack Coulehan

University of Iowa Press  ᴪ  Iowa City

University of Iowa Press,
Iowa City 52242
Copyright © 1998 by the
University of Iowa Press
All rights reserved
Printed in the United States of America
Design by Richard Hendel
http://www.uiowa.edu/~uipress

Library of Congress
Cataloging-in-Publication Data
Blood and bone: poems by physicians /
edited by Angela Belli and Jack Coulehan.
p.  cm.
ISBN 0-87745-637-2, ISBN 0-87745-638-0
(pbk.)
1. Physicians' writings, American.
2. American poetry—20th century.
3. Body, Human—Poetry.
4. Physicians—Poetry.  5. Medicine—
Poetry.  I. Belli, Angela.  II. Coulehan,
Jack.
PS591.P48B58   1998
811'.50809261—dc21            98-7140

98  99  00  01  02  C  5  4  3  2  1
98  99  00  01  02  P  5  4  3  2  1

In memory of John L. Marshall, M.D.

— A. B.

For Rosaly Roffman, Carolyn Page, and Roy Zarucchi,

who helped me discover the poetry in healing.

— J. C.

# Contents

Acknowledgments, xi
Foreword, *Edmund D. Pellegrino*, xiii
Introduction, xv

"FROM PATIENT ONE TO NEXT" 1

Dannie Abse
  *The Doctor*, 5
  *Lunch and Afterwards*, 6
  *Millie's Date*, 7
  *The Stethoscope*, 8
  *Pathology of Colours*, 9
  *X-Ray*, 10
Rafael Campo
  *Her Final Show*, 11
  *S. W.*, 12
  *Towards Curing AIDS*, 13
Ron Charach
  *Labour and Delivery*, 14
  *MRI*, 16
  *The Evidence on Film*, 18
Jack Coulehan
  *D-Day, 1994*, 19
  *The Azalea Poem*, 20
  *I'm Gonna Slap Those
    Doctors*, 21
  *The Man with a Hole in His
    Face*, 22
D. A. Feinfeld
  *Carmelita*, 23
Arthur Ginsberg
  *Stroke*, 24
  *The Chief of Medicine*, 25
John Graham-Pole
  *Candor*, 27
Grace Herman
  *The Clinic*, 28

Eugene Hirsch
  *Two Suffering Men*, 29
Alice Jones
  *Tap*, 31
  *Anorexia*, 32
Jon Mukand
  *Lullaby*, 33
  *First Payment*, 34
Michael O'Reilly
  *abused child*, 36
  *a small girl brings an injured
    bird into the surgery*, 37
  *a house call to a man with
    parkinson's disease*, 39
Frederic W. Platt
  *Coincidentally*, 40
Elspeth Cameron Ritchie
  *Electroconvulsive Therapy*, 41
Vernon Rowe
  *MRI of a Poet's Brain*, 43
  *Time Heals All Wounds — But
    One*, 44
  *Youth*, 45
Audrey Shafer
  *Gurney Tears*, 46
John Stone
  *He Makes a House Call*, 48
  *Confabulation*, 50
Marc J. Straus
  *Luck*, 51

Paula Tatarunis
   *I Have Two Sons and the One I*
     *Love Best Is Robert,* 52
   *Chest X-Ray,* 53
John Wright
   *Therapy,* 54
   *Walking the Dog,* 55

George Young
   *A Letter to William Carlos*
     *Williams,* 56
   *Night Call,* 57

"A DIFFERENT PICTURE OF ME" 59

Rafael Campo
   *El Curandero,* 61
Eric Dyer
   *'Round Killar,* 63
Kirsten Emmott
   *Who Looks after Your Kids?* 64
John Graham-Pole
   *Leaving Mother, 1954,* 65
Alice Jones
   *Communal Living,* 66
Michael Lieberman
   *On the Anniversary of My*
     *Father's Death,* 67
   *Regret,* 68
   *Los Olivos,* 69

Michael O'Reilly
   *potter,* 70
Audrey Shafer
   *Monday Morning,* 72
John Stone
   *The Bass,* 74
   *Rosemary,* 76
   *Talking to the Family,* 79
Marc J. Straus
   *What I Heard on the Radio*
     *Today,* 80
Paula Tatarunis
   *Before the Brain Surgery,* 82
John Wright
   *The Portugal Laurel,* 83
   *Transfiguration,* 84

"IN WAYS THAT HELPED THEM SEE" 85

Dannie Abse
   *Carnal Knowledge,* 88
   *In the Theatre,* 91
   *The Origin of Music,* 93
Rafael Campo
   *What the Body Told,* 94
Robert Coles
   *On Dutch's Death,* 95
Jack Coulehan
   *Anatomy Lesson,* 97
   *The Rule of Thirds,* 98
Eric Dyer
   *Painting the Nude,* 99

D. A. Feinfeld
   *The Wound Man,* 100
James L. Foy
   *Autopsy,* 101
Arthur Ginsberg
   *Line Drive,* 103
John Graham-Pole
   *Venipuncture,* 104
David Moolten
   *Motorcycle Ward,* 105
   *Bio 7,* 107

John Stone
  Gaudeamus Igitur: A
    Valediction, 109

Marc J. Straus
  The Log of Pi, 113
  Neuroanatomy Summer, 114
  Scarlet Crown, 115

## "... THIS WAS THE MUSIC OF OUR LIVES" 117

Louis M. Abbey
  Broken Silence, 120
Ron Charach
  A Question of Vitamins, 122
Robert Coles
  Christmas, Belfast, 124
  The Goddam Street, 126
  New Jersey Boys, 127
Jack Coulehan
  The Dynamizer and the
    Oscilloclast, 129
  Lovesickness: A Medieval Text,
    131
Richard Donze
  Vermont Has a High Suicide
    Rate, 132
Thomas Dorsett
  The Survivor, 134
John Graham-Pole
  The Pain, 135

Norbert Hirschhorn
  Number Our Days, 136
Michael Lieberman
  Prediction, 138
David Moolten
  Voyeur, 139
  Brandy Station, Virginia, 141
  Madame Butterfly, 142
John Stone
  The Truck, 144
  Getting to Sleep in New Jersey,
    146
H. J. Van Peenen
  Will Campbell Displays His
    Craniotribe, 147
  Insulin Receptor, 148
George Young
  Damien, 149
  The Miracle, 151

Permissions, 153
Contributors, 157

# Acknowledgments

For the encouragement and support I have
received in bringing this project into being, I
am grateful to Willard Gingerich, dean of
the Graduate School of Arts and Sciences of
St. John's University.

— A. B.

I'd like to thank Lisa Dougherty, Paula
Viterbo, Catherine Belling, and Peter
Williams for the poetry of their friendship
and the prose of their assistance.

— J. C.

# Foreword

*Edmund D. Pellegrino*

*O happy he whom the Muses love — forth out*
*of his lips sweet words flow.*
*— Hesiod*

It is a common conceit of academics, intellectuals, and sophisticates to believe that physicians as a whole are mere technicians, innocent of arts and letters and insensitive to the life of the mind. Sadly, this impression seems well founded when one listens to the way many physicians expatiate at cocktail and dinner parties. Even when some physician belies this stereotype, he or she is classified as the *rara avis* who by its rarity confirms the original taxonomy.

But that smug taxonomy does not fit the facts. The rare bird is not so rare after all. Physicians, as much as any other group, have been touched by all the Muses of history, painting, writing, music, bibliophilia, etc. Some have been highly talented amateurs in the liberal and fine arts. Others have become medical truants, abandoning Asclepius for one or more of the Muses. With the latter, one thinks immediately of Oliver Goldsmith or John Keats among the poets; of Rabelais, Somerset Maugham, or Walker Percy among the writers of prose; Borodin among the composers; John Locke or Karl Jaspers among the philosophers — to select at random from a rich pool of genius.

Most, however, like William Carlos Williams or Anton Chekhov, remain true to their profession. Medicine and the arts cohabit their lives in symbiotic concord, enriching them as persons and as healers. They are like Hesiod, who was called by the Muses to write the genealogy of the gods. This he did in a thousand hexameters. But later, in his *Works and Days*, he used his gift to transform the story of his life as a farmer into a meditation on the human mysteries of justice. Like Hesiod, most of the physicians in this anthology have remained true to both Asclepius and the Muses. Both their poetry and their art are inextricably grounded in the realities and urgencies of clinical practice.

Through the powers of metaphor, rhythm, rhyme, and meter, these poems transform the mundane world of doctor and patient. Their words evoke levels of empathy with the predicament of illness to which most of us not endowed with the graces of poetry can rarely ascend. Poetry nourishes the poet's soul and emboldens the poet to break the bonds of ordinary logic and language to fathom a little more of the mystery of human healing. Perhaps, as Hesiod and Pindar opined, the poet's "sweet words" themselves may even heal — if not the patient, then the poet.

But the call of the Muses is not without its burdens for Asclepius. Good intentions, good feelings, and facility in rhyming do not themselves make good poetry. Poetic pretension without poetic gifts is a disservice to both medicine and poetry. Shakespeare was blunt about it. Bad poetry he likened to "the forced gait of a shuffling nag." Shelley expressed abhorrence for didactic poetry, a particular temptation for doctors, accustomed as they are to sententious pronouncements. *King Lear* is not a treatise on geriatrics, nor *Othello* on jealousy; yet both teach more about these experiences than the weightiest dissertation because first of all they are good poems. They engage the imagination, opening the door to the mind.

The poems in this collection stand on their own as poetry, whether they speak of the doctor's interaction with a patient, the physician's home life, or the mundaneity of shopping for groceries. In every experience, the poet's vision, sharpened by the doctor's probing eye, lets the hidden light emerge from the most trivial or tragic events. In his acceptance speech on being awarded the Nobel Prize, St.-John Perse set a test for poets: "In these days of nuclear energy can the earthenware lamp of the poet still suffice? Yes, if its clay reminds us of our own." The physician-poets whose work is represented here meet this test. They do indeed remind us of our own clay and of theirs.

We are not as sure as the ancients that poetry was a gift of the gods. Sometimes it appears that Socrates' suspicion that a little madness was involved seems more correct. At other times, we may lean toward some quirk in the human genome to explain what separates the golden-tongued from the poetically mute. But whatever the origin, the gifted poet is a gift to all of us. We who are imprisoned in the prosaic applaud those who dare to break the bonds of prose and lead us deeper into the human soul and condition.

# Introduction

*Angela Belli & Jack Coulehan*

*A wonderful gift! How do*
*you find the time for it in*

*your busy life? It must be a great*
*thing to have such a pastime.*

*But you were always a strange*
*boy. How's your mother?*

— *William Carlos Williams,* Paterson


Imagine William Carlos Williams in his medical office. Sitting at the end of the table is an elderly patient, let's say a woman, a neighbor from Rutherford. She wears a cotton examining gown, tied with a bow at the back of her neck. Doctor Williams is standing beside the table. He places his stethoscope first in one spot on her back and then another, while asking her to breathe through her mouth. Between sibilant coughs, though, she simply can't keep quiet. After all, this is her old friend's son, the famous doctor who writes poetry. "A wonderful gift!" she declares. "How do / you find the time for it in / your busy life?"

In another part of *Paterson*, the narrator — perhaps Everyman, or perhaps the Voice of Reason — makes a stronger comment, a demand, "Give up / the poem. Give up the shilly- / shally of art."

Williams didn't. Nor did he believe that poetry was a strange pastime for a physician. In fact, he found that his medical practice was a spring from which his poems and stories flowed. Medicine and creative writing were inseparable aspects of his life. What brought them so closely together was his consistent attempt to express the "thing" of human relationships, the elusive but deep connection between the self and others, between the self and the world. The means of *seeing* that connection — let us use the artistic and clinical term for it, *empathy* — allows poets to enter into their subject, to celebrate their particularity. An earlier poet, Percy Bysshe Shelley, attributed to poetry a moral dimension precisely because it enabled poets to connect with others. In "A Defence of Poetry" he argues, "A man, to be greatly good, must imagine intensely and comprehensively; he must put himself in the place of another and of many others; the pains and pleasures of his species must become his own. The great instrument of moral good is the imagination and poetry administers to the effect by acting upon the cause." Williams knew that the same way of *seeing* also lies at the heart of physician-patient relationships and the healing connection.

In the 1990s those who shower us with bleak metaphors like "provider" and "gatekeeper" want us to believe that the traditional art of healing is no longer an important part of medical care. At most, the "art" is a thin layer of kindliness that can soften our passage through the world of medical technology. Kindliness, compassion, rapport — sure, they're desirable, the business world tells us, but they're not essential. We have machines to do the work. And management to coordinate the machines. Medicine is science, poetry is art, and never the twain shall meet. Yet every physician who acknowledges uncertainty as a recurring factor in medical practice understands the fallibility of the machine. The unknown, the unexpected may defeat the most advanced technological solution. We can best probe the mysteries of human existence through the uses of the intellect in concert with the imagination. The power of communicating and the sensibility to absorb and transmit intense conceptions regarding humanity and nature reside in the poet, who surpasses the machine by a capability to, in Shelley's words, "measure the circumference and sound the depths of human nature with a comprehensive and all-penetrating spirit."

Beneath the surface, medicine and poetry still draw from the same deep well, first in the act of *seeing* or *paying attention*. Clinical empathy allows a physician to apprehend the patient's values, beliefs, and personal narrative — as a subject rather than as an object composed only of organs and biochemical pathways. At the heart of the medical encounter is also the poetic act of *being with*, simply standing in the presence of suffering. The more one stands in solidarity with ill persons, the more one experiences what cannot be expressed in scientific terms. Medicine also shares the symbolic world of poetry. Healing arises from saying the right words, from performing the right acts. We now understand that in the past unscientific medical therapies were often effective because the patient and physician believed in them, even though the therapies had no "operational" value. Today we tend to view scientific medicine as independent of one's personal beliefs and values. While Native American ceremonies and religious healing practices are effective symbolically, we believe that symbolic healing is no longer necessary in our enlightened age.

Yet, while our American culture tries to convince us that we live only in a world of bodies, everything that is meaningful to us as individuals lies in the world of symbols. The business world is wrong: Medicine cannot be stripped of metaphor, image, symbol, meaning, and interpretation. Ill people experience meaning in their lives and illnesses; they, like all the rest of us, experience themselves as characters in a life narrative; they find in medicine a vast network of healing symbols. Physicians (like poets) manipulate those culturally important symbols. They speak in metaphor. They tell stories. They conduct ceremonies. Thus physicians, like poets, systematically influence others to change their experience by using a kind of liturgy of the word.

Interesting similarities, you might say, but how do they account for this present work, this anthology? Certainly we can't make the claim that physicians ought also to be poets. The vast majority of practitioners neither write poetry nor see their work as particularly poetic. It even seems unlikely that physicians are more inclined to write poetry than people in other jobs or professions — truck drivers, for example, or deli managers, accountants, scientists, or American presidents. The denominator is very large — more than a half million physicians in the United States alone — and the numerator is unknown. The thirty-two fine physician-poets included in this volume may represent nothing more than medicine's share of the small percentage of the general public who write poetry.

While all this is true, it is also true that poetry seems to be thriving in the world of medical publishing. In recent years numerous journals have begun to feature physicians' (and sometimes nonphysicians') poetry on medical subjects. This movement appears to have begun in the 1980s with the weekly "Poetry in Medicine" section of the *Journal of the American Medical Association*. Other journals that currently publish poetry include the *Journal of Family Practice, Annals of Internal Medicine, Lancet, Journal of Medical Humanities, Journal of General Internal Medicine, Pharos, Ambulatory Anesthesia, Mediphors,* and *Western Journal of Medicine.* Most of these venues also feature short stories and personal essays about physicians' experiences.

Our intent in this volume is to harvest the poetry published by physicians in these journals, as well as in more traditional literary magazines and books. Our focus is on the stories and images they present, the questions they ask, the way they approach the world. We want to pose the question: Do physicians bring a particular medical sensitivity to their poetry? Since medical practice is a consuming experience, it is not surprising that most of these poets often choose clinical situations as the subjects for a good number of their poems. Many of them write frequently about professional life. And even when they turn their attention to other aspects of experience, medical terms and concepts may appear in the rendering. But beyond this, is it possible to make a claim for a certain *therapeutic* sensibility in the work of physician-poets? When these men and women write about family or nature or social injustice, is it possible to track the scent of medicine into these distant worlds? And if there is such a therapeutic sensibility in poetry, is it specific to physicians? Or might we also find it in poetry written by nurses, psychologists, or physical therapists?

This anthology represents an attempt to explore these questions by presenting an array of varied and wonderful poems. We wish to acknowledge in advance that the collection is not comprehensive by any means. We reviewed numerous publications and consulted editors and medical humanities teachers. While we tried to gather a representative group of poems by medical practitioners, it is quite likely that we omitted many fine poets whose work we simply don't know. In addition, we had to be selective about the number of poets included because of limitations on the size of the manuscript. We elected, when appropriate, to include several poems by a writer, rather than arbitrarily limiting ourselves to one or two. We hope this will allow the reader to better experience each poet's uniqueness while at the same time exploring his or her works for commonalties.

Near the end of Book 1 in his lovely late poem, "Asphodel, That Greeny Flower," William Carlos Williams wrote:

> It is difficult
> > to get the news from poems
> > > yet men die miserably every day
>
> for lack
> > of what is found there.

In medicine and health care today — perhaps this is a symptom of the 1990s in general — we are worried about getting the news, keeping up to date, changing with the times. But the nourishment of poetry is right there in front of us, at the heart of our daily work.

# "from patient one to next"

The experience of the physician-poet in the professional milieu is the focus of works that probe the interaction between writer and patient or coworker. The poets render portraits of individuals, or tell their stories, or reflect on decisions or courses of action. People of all ages, sometimes loved, sometimes abused, populate these poems. Mood and time change as poets explore diverse relationships. The reader, customarily a vicarious participant, becomes privy to consultations and conflicts between colleagues. Alternately, one's attention is seized by sick and suffering persons whose essence may be fixed either in a moment of crisis or against a backdrop of long association.

One of the most memorable figures to emerge from Dannie Abse's work is the subject of "Millie's Date." Millie, at age 102, has defied the law of averages: She has survived her only child, three husbands, and three wars. White coats surround her bed in awed silence. An unnamed healer is the subject of another Abse poem, "The Doctor." Taking on the dimensions of a type as conceived by his patient, the doctor assumes a much-desired guise. Cheerful and confident, he proceeds to name a curable illness and concoct a potion certain to cure. Never mind that the lie is unchallenged; it counteracts enormous uneasiness.

A rival to Millie for sheer spirit is the subject of Rafael Campo's "Her Final Show," a drag queen dying of AIDS. Sketched in vivid lines, the character maintains her dignity as she gathers strength from the memory of friends who have preceded her in death. At peace with herself, she reaffirms her identity. Equally courageous is the elderly woman of Jon Mukand's "First Payment," who ignores the disease that is ravaging her body to offer a thoughtful gift to the young student who greets her in the examining room. The woman in D. A. Feinfeld's "Carmelita" appears only as a name ballpointed on her jailed boyfriend's chest. The poet must struggle to keep both the girlfriend's identity and the man's life intact as he tries to resuscitate his patient from the stab wound that splits the name in two.

John Stone's "He Makes a House Call" celebrates a warm and enduring physician-patient relationship. The poem takes us back seven years to when the physician "threaded the artery / with the needle" and made a critical diagnosis that saved the patient's life. Inwardly rejoicing at the sight of the woman away from the hospital and on familiar turf, her own garden, he accepts a gift of life from her, an armful of vegetables. A relationship of another kind is intimated in Jon Mukand's "Lullaby." Here the patient is flat in bed, hopelessly ill, all systems failing; the doctor, unable to understand the man's "wheezed-out fragments," imagines cradling the patient in his arms and inserting him into the "clean manila folder" of death.

A disparate bond exists between patient and physician in Eugene Hirsch's "Two Suffering Men." During an office visit, an alcoholic patient berates the man who has diagnosed his problem. Feeling his suffering has not been understood, the patient leaves abruptly — unaware of the vodka hidden in the doctor's desk drawer. In contrast, the patient in Jack Coulehan's "The Man with a Hole in His Face" is passive, devastated at having lost his face to cancer. He expresses a last measure of autonomy by keeping his remaining eye averted from the face of the physician who pesters him with questions. Much more vocal, the patient in Coulehan's "I'm Gonna Slap Those Doctors" has a different take on doctors. They think he is an alcoholic (perhaps he is) and they never listen to what he says. He angrily fantasizes his revenge. He is not so different from the patient in Marc J. Straus's "Luck," who gave up smoking too late and comments ironically on his physician's glib use of the term "luck."

The vitality of eighty-seven-year-old Eulalia, who enjoys telling her story to all within earshot, amuses her doctors, in Frederic W. Platt's "Coincidentally." Remarkable, too, is the main figure in Arthur Ginsberg's "Stroke." She is an eighty-five-year-old whom the reader observes making strenuous, frustrating attempts to communicate with her physician. On his daily visits, the doctor tests and coaxes the woman, marveling at the complexity of her mind, fragmented as it is by catastrophe. He is stunned by her peals of laughter at her own infirmity.

Communication often comes most easily to children, as in the case of the eight-year-old with bone cancer, in John Graham-Pole's "Candor." When told that he is going to die, he first howls, then assesses the situation, lightens up, and offers a joke. A child who can no longer relay fears and pain is the subject of Michael O'Reilly's "abused child." Closing the eyelids of the murdered child, the physician can visualize snowflakes and dreams of ephemeral dancers clinging to the festering corpse.

In Rafael Campo's "S. W." a young woman attempts to mask her husband's abuse by saying she "slipped and struck her face." The husband's behavior, though, and other clues lead the physician to a different conclusion. Nonetheless, it was late at night and what could be done? "I yawned, then offered her / Instructions on the care of wounds. She left." Another young woman, in Alice Jones's "Anorexia," has a cannibalistic relationship to her own body. She scorns the flesh so that she can inhabit a capsule of silk, liquid, and air — sustained only by oranges and water. Grace Herman's "The Clinic" presents a young woman with a breast mass who must listen to the options, not realizing at the time that "not much later, it / runs ahead and takes her with it."

The focus shifts from patients to colleagues in poems such as Campo's "Towards Curing AIDS." Although a patient is present, it is the conflict between physicians or, more precisely, between physicians' rights and responsibilities in caring for AIDS sufferers, that structures the poem. Issues of rank result in conflict between colleagues in Arthur Ginsberg's "The Chief of Medicine" when an intern discovers there is no contest between him and his chief. Protected from the grime of day-to-day patient care, the latter is concerned only with the prompt filing of reports rather than the concerns of the young physician who has just labored the long night through. In Ron Charach's "The Evidence on Film," one colleague is struck by another's obsession. Ever-poised over the subjects of autopsies, a medical photographer patiently keeps adjusting lights, intent to capture on film the soul's escape from the corpse. Lunch with a pathologist occupies Dannie Abse in "Lunch and Afterwards," which juxtaposes the poet's mystical vision of birds of prey consuming a corpse with his colleague's factual account of the progress of decay — recited by rote while he devours his own food.

The most intimate portraits are those of the poets' parents. In "X-Ray" Abse holds his mother's film to the light, unwilling to face the truth it reveals. He contrasts himself to the renowned researchers of the past whose curiosity fueled explorations that led to discoveries and fame. He prefers not to know. The intimate relationship which physicians have with the medical process precludes the bliss of ignorance. Paula Tatarunis knows that she must propitiate the medical gods as she obliges the technician who positions her in "Chest X-Ray." About to be irradiated, she turns her thoughts to Hiroshima and Nagasaki.

Technology provides moments of inspiration for a number of poets. Ron Charach is among them. The subjects in his "MRI" have varied responses to their brush with " high tech," including the speaker of the poem, no braver than the rest, who bluffs his way through the experience. Technology, too, preoccupies the patient in Elspeth Cameron Ritchie's "Electroconvulsive Therapy," which uses the metaphor of the body as a worn-out car, not quite ready for the automobile graveyard. Getting the motor started lowers the mileage. Vernon Rowe takes a different look at modern miracles in "MRI of a Poet's Brain." The astonishing capability of the device for mapping the structure of the brain is tempered by its total uselessness in exposing the formation of a single thought, much less a poem. Sometimes we ask too much of technology. The young man in Coulehan's "D-Day, 1994" suffers from phantom limb pain, having had his arm amputated because of cancer. He wonders whether another diagnostic test, a scan, will reveal the true story of his pain. But the physician, comparing the patient's situation with that of men who lost their limbs in the invasion of Europe, realizes that technology does not have the answer: "You are looking in the wrong place / for an answer." In "Therapy" John Wright, too, urges that we look elsewhere for solutions. Recovery from depression can be achieved not only by medicines and procedures based on scientific data but by enjoying the glories of nature, including the warmth of a comforting hand. In "Walking the Dog" the same poet prescribes another form of healing for an obese patient: a puppy to walk. His gift occasions great glee, but not a healthier lifestyle. The only movement it generates is a good bit of hugging.

Threading his daily way from "patient one to next" in the manner of all his colleagues, George Young identifies with one in particular in "A Letter to William Carlos Williams." The contemporary physician-poet reveals that, like his renowned antecedent, he, too, has uncovered the truth at the core of his professional life: The daily struggle with blood and flesh is a struggle with the self.

# The Doctor

Guilty, he does not always like his patients.
But here, black fur raised, their yellow-eyed dog
mimics Cerberus, barks barks at the invisible,
so this man's politics, how he may crawl
to superiors does not matter. A doctor must care
and the wife's on her knees in useless prayer,
the young daughter's like a waterfall.

Quiet, Cerberus! Soon enough you'll have a bone
or two. Now, coughing, the patient expects
the unjudged lie: "Your symptoms are familiar
and benign" — someone to be cheerfully sure,
to transform tremblings, gigantic unease,
by naming like a pet some small disease
with a known aetiology, certain cure.

So the doctor will and yes he will prescribe
the usual dew from a banana leaf; poppies and
honey too; ten snowflakes or something whiter
from the bole of a tree; the clearest water
ever, melting ice from a mountain lake;
sunlight from waterfall's edge, rainbow smoke;
tears from eyelashes of the daughter.

# Lunch and Afterwards

### Lunch with a pathologist

My colleague knows by heart the morbid verse
of facts — the dead weight of a man's liver,
a woman's lungs, a baby's kidneys.

At lunch he recited unforgettably,
"After death, of all soft tissues the brain's
the first to vanish, the uterus the last."

"Yes," I said, "at dawn I've seen silhouettes
hunched in a field against the skyline, each one
feasting, preoccupied, silent as gas.

"Partial to women, they've stripped women bare
and left behind only the taboo food,
the uterus, inside the skeleton."

My colleague wiped his mouth with a napkin,
hummed, picked shredded meat from his canines,
said, "You're a peculiar fellow, Abse."

DANNIE ABSE

# Millie's Date

With sedative voices we joke and spar
as white coats struggle around her bed.
Millie's 102, all skull; once her head
was lovely — eyes serious, lips ready to be kissed
at Brixham, in "the County of Heaven."
She's outlived three wars and three husbands.
Her only child "passed over," aged 77.

Sometimes she plucks the life-line in her small
left hand; remarks, "An itch means money."
Mostly, though, she's glum or incontinent
with memories. But now, like that immortal
of Cumae who hung in a jar, she cries,
"Let me die, let me die" — silencing us.
How should we reply? With unfunny science?

Or, "Not to worry — the Angels of Death
survive forever"? Often I've wondered
if some are disguised as vagrants, assigned
to each of us and programmed to arrive
punctually for their seedy appointments.
So where's Millie's escort, in which doss-house?
Has he lost his way, has he lost his mind?

Millie's quiet now, in a Valium doze,
and window by window the building darkens
as lights go home. Outside, I half-expect
a doss-house beggar with a violin
to play, "Ah, Sweet Mystery of Life" — some song
like that. Then any passer-by could drop
two coins, as big as eyes, inside his hat.

# The Stethoscope

Through it,
over young women's abdomens tense,
I have heard the sound of creation
and, in a dead man's chest, the silence
　before creation began.

Should I
pray therefore? Hold this instrument in awe
and aloft a procession of banners?
Hang this thing in the interior
　of a cold, mushroom-dark church?

Should I
kneel before it, chant an apophthegm
from a small text? Mimic priest or rabbi,
the swaying noises of religious men?
　Never! Yet I could praise it.

I should
by doing so celebrate my own ears,
by praising them praise speech at midnight
when men become philosophers;
　laughter of the sane and insane;

Night cries
of injured creatures, wide-eyed or blind;
moonlight sonatas on a needle;
lovers with doves in their throats; the wind
　traveling from where it began.

DANNIE ABSE

# Pathology of Colours

I know the colour rose, and it is lovely,
but not when it ripens in a tumour;
and healing greens, leaves and grass, so springlike,
in limbs that fester are not springlike.

I have seen red-blue tinged with hirsute mauve
in the plum-skin of a suicide.
I have seen white, china white almost, stare
from behind the smashed windscreen of a car.

And the criminal, multicoloured flash
of an H-bomb is no more beautiful
than an autopsy when the belly's opened —
to show cathedral windows never opened.

So in the simple blessing of a rainbow,
in the beveled edge of a sunlit mirror,
I have seen, visible, Death's artifact
like a soldier's ribbon on a tunic tacked.

# X-Ray

Some prowl seabeds, some hurtle to a star
and, mother, some obsessed turn over every stone
or open graves to let that starlight in.
There are men who would open anything.

Harvey, the circulation of the blood,
and Freud, the circulation of our dreams,
pried honourably and honoured are
like all explorers. Men who'd open men.

And those others, mother, with diseases
like great streets named after them: Addison,
Parkinson, Hodgkin — physicians who'd arrive
fast and first on any sour deathbed scene.

I am their slowcoach colleague — half-afraid,
incurious. As a boy it was so: you know how
my small hand never teased to pieces
an alarm clock or flensed a perished mouse.

And this larger hand's the same. It stretches now
out from a white sleeve to hold up, Mother,
your X-ray to the glowing screen. My eyes look
but don't want to, I still don't want to know.

# Her Final Show

She said it was a better way to die
Than most; she seemed relieved, almost at peace,
The stench of her infected Kaposi's
Made bearable by the Opium applied
So daintily behind her ears: "I know
It costs a lot, but dear, I'm nearly gone."
Her shade of eyeshadow was emerald green;
She clutched her favorite stones. Her final show
She'd worn them all, sixteen necklaces of pearls,
Ten strings of beads. She said they gave her hope.
Together, heavy as a gallows rope,
The gifts of drag queens dead of AIDS. "Those girls,
They gave me so much strength," she whispered as
I turned the morphine up. She hid her leg
Beneath smoothed sheets. I straightened her red wig
Before pronouncing her to no applause.

# S. W.

Extending from her left ear down her jaw,
The lac was seven centimeters long.
She told me that she slipped and struck her face
Against the kitchen floor. The floor was wet
Because she had been mopping it. I guessed
She'd had to wait for many hours since
The clock read nearly midnight; who mops floors
So late? Her little girl kept screaming in
Her husband's thick, impatient arms: he knocked
Three times, each time to ask when we'd be done.
I infiltrated first with lidocaine.
She barely winced, and didn't start to cry
Until the sixteenth stitch went in and we
Were almost through. I thought my handiwork
Was admirable. I yawned, then offered her
Instructions on the care of wounds. She left.

# Towards Curing AIDS

I slap on latex gloves before I put
My hands inside the wound. A hypocrite
Across the room complains that it's her right
To walk away — to walk away's her right
As a physician. Lapidary, fine,
My patient's eyes are overhearing her.
He doesn't wince. His corner bed inters
Him even now, as she does: he hasn't died,
But he will. The right to treatment medicine
Denied is all the hollows here: along
His arms, the hungry grooves between the bones
Of ribs. As if her surgeon's thread through skin —
The rite of obligation overdue —
Could save him now. I close the wound. The drain
Is repositioned. Needles in his veins,
I leave him pleading. There's too much to do.

# Labour and Delivery

## *When lions are too close*

His wife and he enter
the labour-and-delivery room,
on their minds two wildebeests
more in her loins,
meant for the savannah of birthing
before the lions come.

But the nurse is droning on
about having missed her coffee break
and lays out on the green drape:
two vials of synthetic hormone
two sets of surgical gloves
an amniotomy hook,
then sixteen sets
of surgical clamps,
one for every feeling they came in with
to turn the natural into the man-made,
the man-brought-on.

Is this one more dig
at organized medicine?
Or have they tried too soon,
that backing up that always happens
when lions come too close?

## *You and yours*

When you add a girl
to the boy you have,
to accomplish that miracle
"one of each"
in a family known for few girls;
when the labour's gone smoothly
as such monumental strainings go,
all taken in by dad at his wife's side,

then the fact that next curtain over
in the semiprivate suite
the couple who speak only Ukrainian well
had a baby with a "prolapse of the cord"
now doing badly in Intensive Care
— is just a fact.

No cause to cut into your joy
except for momentary twinges
when you pass them
on visits.

And then that thank-God reflex:
once again the wheel of doom
has not landed on you
or yours.

# MRI

*Nothing left, no more futuristic tests*
*to light up a world of misfiring sensation*
*and surprisingly lasting pain*

In the MR waiting room, gown pants and booties,
a small-town long-hair returns from the test,
"It was nothin' —" he brags, "— like bein' *inside* a Pink Floyd CD."
But the elderly lady said,
"Those MRI's are the worst."

Questioned for rings, watch,
recent operations' clips, pacemakers —
I'm rollered into a cool-white plastic chamber,
a huge laundromat dryer, wind tunnel
with only a few inches'
clearance for face trunk and arms,
claustrophobia,
prematurial burial.
I await the draw of The Magnets,
their Holstian 50,000 times stronger than gravity
to line up all my hydrogen atoms,
bombard me with radio frequencies
and scan every change.
*Magnetic Resonance Imaging*
photos as perfect, as cadaverous
as those in the *Atlas of Anatomy.*

I wear earphones.
Already I've known the CT Scan,
its crazed drumbeats followed by
ten thousand pounds of hamburger grinding.

The technician warned:
"You'll hear knocking noises, then a drilling sound
that will last one to four minutes.
There will be knocks like premonitions,
then an electroshock *vibrando* will shake you to your core
and redefine 'heart-throb,' 'incessant' and 'compelling.'

You'll breathe at ever-higher volumes
without *daring* to move, waiting for the
hovering craft to leave.
Think of your body as a tooth
encountering a five-story drill.
Think of this as your biggest-ever brush
with high tech."

After the longest minutes life offers,
I vow to refuse the next fifteen.
Yet when they wheel me out
and ask "How ya doing?"
I answer, "Nothin' beats it."

# The Evidence on Film

Here's a live one,
works in medical photography
Not a bad job — short and solitary hours
with all the skin you can see
though much of it is geriatric
or looks like liver
for one reason or another.
You can afford not to be idealistic
he says.
I can afford; I can afford;
I work down in X-ray;
I know I'm slowly being baked
— I keep my back to the machine at times
so I'm done the same
both sides; the chance of having a kid
with five fingers on each hand
is probably one in ten.
But back to Mr. Medical Photography;
all alone in his dark room
with the stages of the autopsy,
*Ooga-Booga!*
You could jump him
like the bony hand of death itself
while he's leaning over a stillborn child on a drape.
But you wouldn't want to:
His hair is soft,
his eyes lit green by the lamps,
waiting for something to develop;
he really believes
that if the lighting's right
he'll catch the soul escaping.

JACK COULEHAN

# D-Day, 1994

Your arm is gone
to cancer at 30 — no honor
in that. The potato-like stump
is not where the pain is.

You take your pills
and watch TV —
where beaches in France
swim with images of old men
pacing the coast for the first time
since going down.

You notice their limps
and imagine the vacancies —
fear, lost limbs, their buddies dead.
Who would have thought
the first tide of grunts
attacking that fortified coast
could win the war?

You ask if a scan would explain
the pain in your phantom limb,
believing a scan is like a story
that reveals things. Those men
creeping the grey-crossed breast
of a hill on the coast of France —
they know what they lost, they know
what they are looking for.

The scan will not give you an answer.
You are looking in the wrong place
for an answer. The world works hard
to hide its d-day —
deception, danger, death,
deliverance. I wish I could give you
the old men's stories. I wish I could give you
their battles, which are almost used up
but still true.

# The Azalea Poem

The hope I handed Alfred
when he asked about his skin
seems so cheaply false
since I came home,
so quick, so colored by my need.

And my workout
on the weight machine
to Mahler's Third was not
what I had hoped for. My form,
which has always had the urge
to be a pear, is sour
and inelastic. How nylon-light
my youth would be
if I were living it today!

Alfred's young.
Last month a vivid growth
between his toes
spoke line and verse. This month
his legs
are smoldering with death.

I used to wish whole clots of time
would disappear.
In another month, my madness told me,
I'd reach my next goal
and be happier. Between the points —
tedious fiber.

Today is a taste of heaven,
Alfred said.
Just cooking supper for Tom, he said.
The breath of woods behind our house
is what it's like, he told me
and asked if he would live to see
azalea bloom. And I said, yes.

JACK COULEHAN

# I'm Gonna Slap Those Doctors

Because the rosy condition
makes my nose bumpy and big,
and I give them the crap they deserve,
they write me off as a boozer
and snow me with drugs. Like I'm gonna
go wild and green bugs are gonna
crawl on me and I'm gonna tear out
their goddamn precious IV.
I haven't had a drink in a year
but those slick bastards cross their arms
and talk about sodium. They come
with their noses crunched up like my room
is purgatory and they're the
goddamn angels doing a bit
of social work. Listen, I might not
have much of a body left,
but I've got good arms — the polio
left me that — and the skin on my hands
is about an inch thick. And when I used
to drink I could hit with the best
in Braddock. Listen, one more shot
of the crap that makes my tongue stop
and they'll have something on their hands
they didn't know existed. They'll have time
on their hands. They'll be spinning around
drunk as skunks, heads screwed on backwards,
and then Doctor Big Nose is gonna smell
*their* breaths, wrinkle *his* forehead, and spin
down the hall in his wheelchair
on the way to the goddamn heavenly choir.

JACK COULEHAN

# The Man with a Hole in His Face

He has the lower part,
a crescent of face
on the right, and an eye

that sits precipitously
beside the moist hole
where the rest of his face was.

The hole is stuffed
with curls of gauze.

His nurse comes before dawn, ·
at the moment
the eye fears for its balance,

and fills the wound,
sculpting a tortured landscape
of pack ice.

The man's eye does not close
because any blink
is death,

nor does the eye rest
in mine
when I ask the questions
he is weary of answering.

While I wait here quietly
in arctic waste,
the pack ice cracks
with terrifying songs.

Over the moist hole
where the rest of his face was,
he rises.

This man is the man in the moon.

# Carmelita

The first time I see
*CARMELITA*
tattooed on your left breast
in Gothic letters ballpointed
by a jailhouse artist
you stick your chest out
tell me where to hear your heart
behind the blue-black word
proud your girl will wait
you happily paid the scribe
twenty cartons of Luckies

The next time I see
*CARMELITA*
the *E* is split in two
by a six-inch steel shank
and I press Carmelita's name
every second with my palm
to force your blood-choked heart
back from the drying river
where your mind
is losing its memory
of the girl who would wait
after your Luckies were spent

# Stroke

Comes down, white as an avalanche,
erasing the playground of speech,
piles up in a drift at the tip
of Veida's tongue. She cannot repeat,
*no ifs, ands, or buts*, calls a comb,
bone, pen, cow. Frustration bleeds
through her brokenness, shudders in
chaotic clutching of spindly fingers,
as if the right word could be plucked
from air. *Veida, Veida, listen to me.*
*Follow my hand with your eyes.* Eyes
brimming, she nods and follows, pendulum
on command. Stroke pitches camp,

lays rebar, pours cement. She grows to
know me and I, her, without ancestral
gift; small patch of brain, ordered as
the stars. From bedside, touch speaks,
vision flows in syllables, unfettered as
a child skipping rope. Fingertips vibrate
loquaciously as lips, extolling all the hope
of eighty-five years; married to darling Jack,
librarian, rebuilding spines of orphaned books.

Stroke binds her in the vault of our audacious
builder, pitiless as, buried alive. I visit Veida
each day, stunned by peals of laughter at
her own infirmity, that come from cosmic space,
roiling up through ghostly cracks to pry open,
the lock. Waylaid by walls, eyes fade, no word
to frame, good-bye. Undoing speaks to
the marvel of design, more eloquent
than speech, the vespers of silence.

# The Chief of Medicine

Anton Steiner sits behind a rosewood desk
in the ivory tower across the street from
Armageddon. I stand before him, buck private
intern, drenched in sweat and grime, after
48 hours of emergency duty. He demands
a bill of lading; handwritten cards on seventy
Brooklyn souls in various stages of entropy.
As if I had just disembarked from a European
trip, brightly coloured postcards following
obediently in my wake. He has not seen
seventy humans spread like a mosaic beneath
stethoscope and rubber-gloved hands. I want
to say, I am fatigued and my feet ache, that
I don't give a damn for documentation, that
I want to sleep and shower, the way he did
before work. I want to say, the cards will not
tell José Martinez's story, how he died in
my arms, a steak wedged in his windpipe. How,
my own esophagus quivers on the verge
of spasm. He listens impassively as dust,
the metal of his eyes, dead as glacial blue.
He has forgotten the feel of membranes, slick
in a split-open chest, putrefaction from an addict's
abcess, the *all clear* shouts before paddles
convulse a skewered heart. The cards will not
say why Dora, bag-lady from Flatbush, thinks
I am her reincarnated son from Jerusalem, will
not recapture one iota of my pleasure, when
I cut through Amber's pantyhose, to reveal
the glistening head of her newborn son. Or,
horror of a man who screwed himself with
a lightbulb, forgetting glass is fragile. I want to
tell Steiner, these cards are old news, that
the ink was spilled hours ago, that the ink
ran like blood to my knees and elbows, that
the world is strangling in ink and paper,

that electronic patterns on oscilloscopes
are something we have invented to remove
us from matters of the heart. He says in
mellifluous voice, *the report is due by nine,*
my future depends on it, *that is all.*

# Candor

At eight years old, his cancer running rampage,
Joe perches on my office sofa edge
thigh-to-thigh with mom
(who has enjoined me: "Square with him").

But I beat about the bush a bit,
then come at last to it: "Joey:
you're going to die, go to heaven."
Words lost in his howl, like a wolf's,

the hurling of his body into
the yellow print dress's recesses.
Three minutes at least of this, this keaning,
while we eye each other, panicked:

whatever else was right to do this wasn't it.
Then, as instantly, at a long-drawn-in
breath's end, he stops, swivels out, flicks a look,
spots tears on cheeks of mom, dad, nurse, me,

determines he's grieved enough. Time to
lighten up, knowing me at other times a joker,
a wearer of odd socks, funny noses. He spies
memos, charts, photocopies, journals —

jetsam of an urgent life — scattering my carpet,
and becomes the stand-up comic,
offering his own joke: "Didn't your mom
tell you to pick up after yourself?"

# The Clinic

*for Sharon Washington*

She tells us she felt
the lump three days ago.
Here it is,
visible, in her left breast.
Here she is,
pale, slender, thirty.

We feel it, in turn, think
and say, probably a cyst.
She smiles. But, we say,
you should see someone,
give her a name. She goes.

It's not simple. We know
when no attempt is made
to aspirate, the x-
ray suspicious.

Where to go, what to do.
We talk: two doctors,
the patient, her mother.

And soon, not much later, it
runs ahead and takes her with it.

EUGENE HIRSCH

# Two Suffering Men

I sat across, behind my desk,
and told him I thought
he might be alcoholic.
"I never been drunk," he said.
I made a note on the medical chart.

I could see him getting irked.
His liver sick;
his wife gone with the kids!
I made a note on the chart.

I saw him gaining rage.
He clenched his fists,
leaned forward,
his arms on the desk.
He held his breath
until he turned red,
then, sighing, fell back
in his chair and cried.

Breaking a long pause,
he asked, "You're telling me
I'm alcoholic? How in hell
would you know, in your
'pretty' white picturebook
middle-class hospital coat?"
His face suddenly tensed.
He pursed his lips
and lifted himself from the chair.
He stood tall, straight up,
bulging with pride
for all the ground-in years
of his laboring trade,
shouting,
"Stay out of my head.
Stay OUT of my head!"
and slammed the door behind him.

I longed to lower my eyes and cry.
But, from the bottom drawer
of my desk, just one small glass
of vodka and a chlorophyll candy
taste so damn good in the morning.

# Tap

I love to find a door. Like the spinal tap —
above the draped fetal curve, you work
the trocar inwards. Dowser, boatman,
auger, bore. Every surface has its opening,
even bone. Steel finds fossa, penetrates.
That give, as the needle enters dura.
Slide out the central metal filament,
it rings, and the invisible emerges, drop
by drop, caught in transparent tubes. So

much fineness — glass and silver, the white
field, crystalline fluid. Seek and you find.
How it comes, the brain's clear bath.

ALICE JONES

# Anorexia

Not everyone is so skilled
at the ancient art, not everyone
can exist on air, refusing
the burden of flesh. Hating

the yellow globs of fat in any
form — under the skin, padding
the heart, cushions for the eye's
globes, but mostly those

that mark her as her mother's —
the encumbering curves of hip
or breast, she eats only
oranges and water, a cannibal

of self. Trying to undo all
the knots the female body has
tied, all the cyclical obligations,
to gush, to feed, she chooses

to hone her shape down,
her scapulae prepared like
thin birds, to fly away from
the spine. Barely held together

by silk and liquid and air,
she floats, flightless, the water's
iciness along her back;
she tries not to be sucked

down by the black cold,
its deadliness pulling
at the nape of her long neck,
biting at her unfeathered heels.

JON MUKAND
# Lullaby

Each morning I finish my coffee,
And climb the stairs to the charts,
Hoping yours will be filed away.
But you can't hear me,
You can't see yourself clamped
Between this hard plastic binder:
Lab reports and nurses' notes, a sample
In a test tube. I keep reading
These terse comments: stable as before,
Urine output still poor, respiration normal.
And you keep on poisoning
Yourself, your kidneys more useless
Than seawings drenched in an oil spill.
I find my way to your room
And lean over the bedrails
As though I can understand
Your wheezed-out fragments.
What can I do but check
Your tubes, feel your pulse, listen
To your heartbeat insistent
As a spoiled child who goes on begging?

Old man, listen to me:
Let me take you in a wheelchair
To the back room of the records office,
Let me lift you in my arms
And lay you down in the cradle
Of a clean manila folder.

# First Payment

In the waiting room, she releases
her white hair from a blue gauze scarf.
Her body has accepted the disease with
no cure, her questions are
empty snail shells. The pain stays,
with the appetite of crabgrass.
She cannot reach
inside, pluck it out by the roots.

Some days, she wants to be only
a gust of winter wind sweeping
the fresh snow
into drifts & whorls on the prairie, filtering
through an apple orchard. She might
linger, wrap herself around
naked branches, wait for spring buds.
She might even learn to be
patient for the orange sun
to drag the bleached skeleton of each day
behind the snow-tinted hills.

The intercom calls. Clenching her
body, she lifts herself up
with a gnarled, polished walkingstick.
In the examining room, her eyes
wander over the fresh table,
the chrome lamp with its fixed gaze.

The student knocks and enters, ready
for her coerced smiles, her
handshake brittle as a curled-up leaf.
From her black handbag, a
sealed envelope. Open it.
Inside, a new fifty-dollar bill.
To help with school, I know it's expensive.
He can only smile, return her money.
It lies in her palm like a

handful of earth picked up, raised
to the sky
as an offering to the spring wind.

# abused child

*for Sorcha, aged 6*

you dreamt of being a dancer, but frightened
of being found out, and beaten, you made a
batik secret of all the colours you never knew, and hung it
like a backdrop in case
they held auditions for love;
but they didn't, so, unable to catch the snowflakes
in your sleep, when he came
to hurt you or just break
the watersbone beneath your blistered feet, the ballet ended
with the poems and curtain calls i could not reach you with.
the policeman said
you were "inconsistent with life" when they found you
almost unburned
of all this innocence, this tiny stain
that may have been marks of lips
or the wing-prints of pain
that beat out against you like a Kallimba.
and the pus that oozes
from your scraped eyes was the colour of jonquil
sea horses
washed ashore,
like tiny envois of peace to tell you
it would soon be over.
they have called me to close your eyelids
down
like awnings on this day i found you
dead, festered, beaten, stung,
all along the insides of your dancer's legs
where, between the marks of lips and
the wing-prints of pain,
the snowflake fell

the batik hung.

MICHAEL O'REILLY

# a small girl brings an injured bird into the surgery

*from a city-centre practice*

march, now, and almost the season,
when all the broken promises no one kept for you
will be washed up with the sewage on our city beaches
and snow,
snared in the cold reeds along the shore, like fireworks,
will burn when you touch it.

it was only a small bird, when you found it, hit by a coal truck,
resting by crippled wings as if sent
to understand the hidden sanskrit in your tearful eyes,
"can you fix him, doctor?" you ask me, and i
wonder how fragile you might have been
before they broke you, abandoned you
to grow up with the absence-seizures you try
and keep secret until
you bring its tiny stilled body in, ask me to save it
with petit-mal prayers
and then i know.

maybe the memory of the sound, the slight thud, its
bloodied feathers strewn across your troubled sleep will remind you
of the sirens screaming through
your block of flats, the smell
of burning syringes will shell you of
this intimate
peaceful,
caring.

"get out of this surgery with that bird, this isn't a zoo!"
the secretary shouts at you and you run outside
crying;
child, they will hurt you, when i was
a boy i found three fox cubs with gunwounds
in our barley field with their dead mother
and could not save them.

and i am learning to be a doctor, now, to pass
dying children by

because they have burnt me at the catherine-wheel.

MICHAEL O'REILLY

# a house call to a man with parkinson's disease

*for mr sexton, and his wife*

you must have
loved her once, i can tell
by the photograph dusted light as
candlemoths she keeps
by the window
where you sit, drifting alone
against the caudate's slick undertow
and
you only see her sometimes,
the doctor asks me
do i notice your pill-rolling tremor, your
classical
vacant stare, "no need for a scan, the signs are there" he says,
and you look a little confused at the lady
with the gray hair
who has just
held your hand for
hours, washed your face, read you
the news from a war almost
as fierce
as the one inside your head.
she lifts you
to bed, pretending
on the children
you never gave her;

a little white line of crosses buried
in a cemetery near her heart
no sign
would show,

and when you smile for her, the flowers bloom beneath the snow.

# Coincidentally

She wants me to hear the whole story
whether I am interested or not.

"You see, it was like this,
I was lying in bed this morning
and I said to myself, Eulalia,
you have just had your 87th birthday.
You better make an appointment to go in
and let that Dr. Anneberg check you over
from your head down to your toes,
when all of a sudden, there welled up
in my throat a mouthful of blood."
She got up to spit it out and was amazed
not so much by the strange and frightening
event itself, as by the coincidence
of thinking of her doctor just then.
"I was thinking of him, you see,
not a moment before.
I don't ordinarily,
but I did today."

Bemused, I too enjoy hearing her
tell it all over again to the next doctor
in line, as we arrange for a quick look
into her innards.
"Yes," I say,
"quite a coincidence."

ELSPETH CAMERON RITCHIE

# Electroconvulsive Therapy

This motor won't start.

My mate takes me
to the hospital, again.
Why? Drugs don't work.
My mouth is dry, bowels
clogged, brain slow,
singed heart falters.
Life is shot.

I wish I could fade
into a junkyard,
with other carcasses of
colonels and cars.

Electricity, doctors insist.
They want to jump-start me.
They should give up,
hang up their cables,
like the noose I dream of.

How can a seizure help?
Again wife and daughters plead.
We are destined to failure;
I finally yield.

They wheel me down,
put a plastic mask on
my face, drugs in weakened
veins. I smell apples.

Four more times: dreams
of stockcars and winning,
and, they say, convulsions.
The scent of fruit, and
the buzz of honeybees
return to me.

My brain begins to rev,
the starter motor works;
we used to neck in my T-bird.
I feel my sex jumping.

VERNON ROWE

# MRI of a Poet's Brain

In this image
of your brain
I see each curve
in the corpus callosum,
curlicues of gyri,
folding of fissures,
sinuous sulci,
mammillary bodies,
arcuate fasciculus,
angular gyrus,
tracts and nuclei,
eyes and ears,
tongue and pharynx,

but not even
a single syllable
of one
tiny
poem.

# Time Heals All Wounds — But One

He was a huge
hulk of a man
but the blade cut his belly
like it was a melon.
He was cheerful at first
but as weeks wore on
like his cheap shoes
and time spun out
with miles of gauze packing,
his wound stank
and Leroy shrank
shriveled nearly
to skin and skeleton.
One day, barely
conscious, he whispered:
"Let me go, Doc,"
and I did.

VERNON ROWE

# Youth

She glided into
the office, lavender,
brilliant, springtime,
blonde. Her eyes
clear, hopeful
in the face
of fear.

The only things betraying
her seventy-two years
were a few wrinkles
and a minimal tremor,
and we can fix those.

AUDREY SHAFER

# Gurney Tears

Morning frost cocoons my car.
I drive anyway
      peeping through the hole widened
            by hot air and the slash of wipers.

The physician
      excises, exonerates, exhorts
      a vertical parasite on the supinated.
Yet, even so,
A patient will gently
      push aside the doctor's probing fingers,
Reach in, and produce his own
Soul, which he holds out on his palm
a gleaming light
a sudden clarification
Before he collects himself and pockets it back inside.

Today is a day of gurney tears
      glistening in canthi or lingering in the hollow between cheek
    and tragus.
I see fluorescent lights mirrored on the liquid
      taste salt on my mind's tongue.

The mother of three
Embarrassed, cries before her sterilization.
Tears dampen her black hair.
She smiles, apologizes.
How difficult the letting
go.
The quiet flow continues till she drifts into anesthesia.

The internist, whose coronary artery grafts
      prematurely close,
Forces his tears inward
      falling
      like rain dropping into hollow pots.
      — *They were supposed to last ten years*

He mutters over and over
        and is drenched in raw, uncontrollable sweat.

And finally — the veteran who had survived
War, operations, pain
        today is defeated by the dry suck of cigarettes
The first leg will be amputated.
He shakes the gurney with sobs
        before his piecemeal death.
Only forty-five, he is already white-whiskered —
        they look soft
I want to touch them.
Instead I touch his hand, then inject into his intravenous line.

I am swollen. I need time
        apart.
It's getting cold.
Almost home.
Perhaps it will snow tonight
        and I can sleep
                under the white, white covers.

# He Makes a House Call

Six, seven years ago
when you began to begin to faint
I painted your leg with iodine

threaded the artery
with the needle and then the tube
pumped your heart with dye enough

to see the valve
almost closed with stone.
We were both under pressure.

Today, in your garden,
kneeling under the sticky fig tree
for tomatoes

I keep remembering your blood.
Seven, it was. I was just
beginning to learn the heart

inside out.
Afterward, your surgery
and the precise valve of steel

and plastic that still pops and clicks
inside like a Ping-Pong ball.
I should try

chewing tobacco sometimes
if only to see how it tastes.
There is a trace of it at the corner

of your leathery smile
which insists that I see inside
the house; someone named Bill I'm supposed

to know; the royal plastic soldier
whose body fills with whiskey
and marches on a music box

"How Dry I Am";
the illuminated 3-D Christ who turns
into Mary from different angles;

the watery basement,
the pills you take, the ivy
that may grow around the ceiling

if it must. Here, you
are in charge — of figs, beans,
tomatoes, life.

At the hospital, a thousand times
I have heard your heart valve open, close.
I know how clumsy it is.

But health is whatever works
and for as long. I keep thinking
of seven years without a faint

on my way to the car
loaded with vegetables
I keep thinking of seven years ago

when you bled in my hands like a saint.

# Confabulation

Striding up to his bed, you
know the right questions.
Old with alcohol, yellow
as a lemon, he wrinkles

for a cigarette. He
will lie to you at a moment's
confusion, going along with you

to cover the fact that he can't
remember yesterday.

Do you remember me?

*Sure I remember you.*

We met in the bar at 8th
and Jackson.

*Yeah, sure.*

The redhead: you remember her?

*Yeah, I remember.*

What was her name — started with
an *L* . . .

*Loretta? Laura?*

Loretta. That's it. What a
woman. You're a lucky man to
know Loretta.

*I know. I know Loretta. I'm a lucky man.*

And Loretta is a lucky woman.

# Luck

Just my luck. I gave up smoking last month
and the doctor says there's a lesion in my lung.

If I'm lucky, he says, it'll be curable.
I tell him the T.V. showed two kids rescued

from a burning building and the reporter said
it's lucky they're alive. So I say, how come

it's lucky they got second-degree burns. How come
they were in the building in the first place.

Want to hear about real luck, I say. I have this itch
under my arm. I'll scratch it twice in slow circles

and the lesion in my lung is gone.

PAULA TATARUNIS

# I Have Two Sons and the One I Love Best Is Robert

Why she should trouble her young
doctors with her filial preference
is as mysterious as that Other Son,

the one left out of her utterance,
except as a black shadow
that slides and folds

limber as a vampire's cape
along the strange brick walls
of her senility.

That's the shadow that follows us now,
who tags along from bed to bed
like some doppelganger intern

who majored in
autopsies, melancholia
and diseases of the spleen;

and who, on his lonely midnight rounds,
devours like a famished wolf
all the withered get-well fruit he can find

rotting on the hospital window sills:
the unacceptable sacrifices
of all the Other Sons.

# Chest X-Ray

She adjusts my hip, spine, shoulder
against the roentgen plate. Note
my waxy flexibility
is so perfect
it might have been borrowed
from a catatonic!

I am so well behaved and chaste
in my lead apron
and Cerenkov-blue gown:
there are medical gods to propitiate
with lumberjack appetites —
meat and potato men,
trenchermen, gourmands —

so when she tells me to take a deep breath
and hold it without swaying
I clasp my hands on my head
as if praying
for a schooldesk
and inkpot to descend.
And I wait.
This is how prisoners of war stand,
obedient, afraid, elbows forward,
ready to cast
their gamma shadow anywhere,

just as I am standing here
in this little August *entre-deux-guerres*
holding my crouched heart
in its slatted cage,
bird and refugee,
right between the eyes
of Hiroshima and Nagasaki.

JOHN WRIGHT

# Therapy

*for Philip*

You attribute my recovery
to *nor trip tyline* —
its effect on neurotransmitters,
on the *a myg dala.*

You barely nod towards your worth —
insisting on blood levels,
on a therapeutic dose.

While I credit half our success
to the pear tree blossoming white
beyond your left shoulder,

to the wisteria —
its pink flowers hanging
lush and fragrant
over the portico,

to the warmth of your hand.

JOHN WRIGHT
# Walking the Dog

She weighed
three hundred pounds.
Fat and high sugars
were killing her
I thought.

So,
I thought.
So,

I gave her a puppy
with dark curly hair,
nothing else
had worked.

Walking the dog
twice a day
I thought
might persuade,
might motivate.

She was pleased
with my prescription,
she laughed,
she rocked
from side to side.

She lived
for twelve years
hugging
that little black dog
while her lean husband
walked it faithfully,
twice a day.

# A Letter to William Carlos Williams

We know, Doctor Williams, you and I,
as we go
from patient one to next,
thumb
the rumpled charts, cough
nervously and look away from worried eyes,
what
we will see —

What is, is, and it is
just this: the
truth
of blood and flesh we wrestle with:
sheer, brute, singular,
wounded —

ourselves.

# Night Call

Sunday night, 2:00 A.M.,
I'm driving home through a dark town.
In my headlights it's snowing.
The ambulance, its red light
streaking the snow, brought her in
unconscious from the nursing home.
When she stopped breathing, the ER Doc
intubated her. "Probably a mistake,"
he said. Later in the waiting room
I confronted her family, dairy farmers
with vacant eyes. "There is no hope,"
I said. "She's had a massive stroke."
I returned to the ER and nodded to the nurse
who was squeezing the ambu bag, "Let's stop!"
But green blips still marched across
the cardiac monitor, and after a minute
she gasped and began to breathe on her own.
So I admitted her to the hospital.
"We'll have to wait," I told them. "But I know
she wouldn't want a *machine*." We all agreed:
ninety-nine years is a long time.
And now I'm driving home. The town
is empty. The snow is falling down.

# "a different picture of me"

Away from hospital or office, usually at home, writers reveal a different aspect of themselves. They explore the private world of personal relationships in contrast to the professional world. At times the connection between the two appears remote. At other times one world impinges swiftly and unexpectedly upon the other.

Enjoying a peaceful moment at home, Marc J. Straus makes a rare diagnosis — one without a patient present — in "What I Heard on the Radio Today." Between the notes of a Horowitz recording of Schumann made in 1928, the poet detects the sound of a man coughing. The quality of the cough, coupled with his physician's knowledge and experience, enables him to determine the nature of the disease, its progress and consequences for the invisible cougher, now long dead. It is at home, too, that John Wright learns that his capacity to feel has not diminished after decades of relegating tears to the pockets of his long white coat. In "The Portugal Laurel" he describes being pierced by sadness upon viewing the "weeping stump" of a favorite tree that he has had to remove from his property. Yet he knows that tomorrow the "pale blue numbness" that he experiences today will be gone.

The comforts of home enable the physician in Rafael Campo's "El Curandero" to enjoy respite from his public obligations. As he enjoys a warm bath, he sees reflected in the glazed tiles about him "a different picture of me." Shedding his professional identity, he unburdens himself of the oppressing moments of his day at the hospital by surrendering himself to an invisible healer — "He is in the steam, / So he can touch my face" — whose soothing, revitalizing power springs from his Hispanic culture.

John Stone's experience on a fishing trip with his son, related in "The Bass," reinforces his physician's knowledge that death is inescapable, often unexpected. His two worlds intersect in the image of the fishing trophy resting on his desk. In "Talking to the Family," Stone takes us to his office in the hospital where a "white coat waits in the corner / like a father." With the coat on, he must deliver bad news that will change a family's life. But when he doffs the coat, he enters a different world, becomes a different person. He will "drive home, / and replace the light bulb in the hall."

An encounter of the nonscientific kind between a physician and a stripper in a local nightspot begins to look suspiciously like a physician-patient meeting once the stripper discovers the man's professional identity in Eric

Dyer's "'Round Killar." The dancer is intent on procuring only medical advice, much to the chagrin of the physician. On a more serious note, Michael O'Reilly in "potter" and Paula Tatarunis in "Before the Brain Surgery" find that their intimate moments with loved ones are marred by the intrusion of crucial health concerns for their partners.

Kirsten Emmott deals humorously with the serious issue of the conflicting demands of career and family in "Who Looks after Your Kids?" To the critics who would judge her according to their standards, she shoots back flippant answers to their endless interrogation. Softer in tone, Audrey Shafer's "Monday Morning" touches on the same issue. Prepared to start her week at work, the woman is dressed, beepered, and on her way, until stopped at the door by her three-year-old son. The aura of his "just-awakened warmth" accompanies her into the operating suite as she prepares to put a patient to sleep.

A boy's permanent separation from his mother is foreshadowed in John Graham-Pole's "Leaving Mother, 1954." The poet captures a healthy child's blissful unawareness of illness and death as he enjoys a romp in the woods with his mother before her death. The work fixes in time the last carefree moment that mother and son will experience together. A son's memory of his father emerges from Michael Lieberman's "On the Anniversary of My Father's Death." The poem is from a son who has permitted the daily concerns of a busy life to obscure his filial obligations. Belatedly, he performs for his deceased father the rites he owes him.

Looking back, Alice Jones re-creates in "Communal Living" an instant of past experience shared by light-hearted friends spending time together in a rural setting. Convinced of the immortality of their youth, they would surely have been thrown into fits of laughter at any prophesy of their future — a future that would include loss, deprivation, and early death for some. For one it would include medical school.

RAFAEL CAMPO

# El Curandero

I am bathing. All my greyness —
The hospital, the incurable illnesses,
This headache — is slowly given over
To bathwater, deepening it to where

I lose sight of my limbs. The fragrance,
Twenty different herbs at first (dill, spices
From the Caribbean, aloe vera)
Settles, and becomes the single, warm air

Of my sweat, of the warmth deep in my hair —
I recognize it, it's the smell of my pillow
And of my sheets, the closest things to me.
Now one with the bathroom, every oily tile

A different picture of me, every square
One in which I'm given the power of curves,
Distorted, captured in some less shallow
Dimension — now I can pray. I can cry, and he'll

Come. He is my shoulder, maybe, above
The grey water. He is in the steam,
So he can touch my face. Rafael,
He says, I am your saint. So I paint

For him the story of the day: the wife
Whose husband beat purples into her skin,
The jaundiced man (who calls me Ralph, still,
Because that's more American), faint

Yellows, his eyes especially — then,
Still crying, the bright red a collision
Brought out of its perfect vessel, this girl,
This life attached to, working, the wrong thing

Of a tricycle. I saw pain —
Primitive, I could see it, through her split
Chest, in her crushed ribs — white-hot. Now,
I can stop. He has listened, he is silent.

When he finally speaks, touching my face,
It sounds herbal, or African, like drums
Or the pure, tiny bells her child's cries
Must have been made of. Then, somehow,

I'm carried to my bed, the pillow, the sheets
Fragrant, infinite, cool, and I recognize
His voice. In the end, just as sleep takes
The world away, I know it is my own.

# 'Round Killar

This stripper is dancing
and doing much worse
on this round table so close,
then comes and sits by *me*.

All I can think to say
is "Thank you"
and, of course,
"A drink for Killar, please."

Pretty soon I learn
she is a CPA from Jacksonville,
and I tell her I am
a doctor here in town.

Then one thing leads
to another, and soon
I am palpating this
large, soft, round flesh

on the back of her head,
and my heart is pounding
as she lifts her hair
like a skirt to show me

her domed, sebaceous cyst
occipitally concealed,
and I know at that moment
that I am a square.

# Who Looks after Your Kids?

"Who looks after you kids while you work?"
"Who does the housework?"
"How do you manage working those long hours with a family?"
"How do you manage with the kids?"

Well, there's their father, and a nanny and a day-care centre.
But they don't really hear.
They don't want to know about it.

What they want to hear is:

Who does the housework? My henpecked worm of a husband. Me,
until four in the morning. A Jamaican wetback whom I blackmail
into working for peanuts. Nobody, we all live in a huge tattered
ball of blankets like a squirrel's nest.

Who bakes the bread?   Never touch it.   Mac's Bakery.   The pixies.
A little Irishwoman named Kirsten Emmott comes in every week.

How do you manage with the kids? I don't. I neglect them. I'm
on the verge of a nervous breakdown, please help me. I'm
drinking heavily. I don't give a damn about the kids, let them go
to hell their own way.

Who looks after the kids? Nobody, I tie them to a tree in the
back yard all day. My senile old grandmother. The Wicked Witch
of the West.

JOHN GRAHAM-POLE

# Leaving Mother, 1954

*On a last tramp through Weston Woods before her death*

We slipped, trampled, tripped
on oak roots and knots poked
through a mat of burned-brown
pine thorn and rotting conker
autumn damp in august;

we little ones casting away the
littler ones that flew at us,
as if casting off spells that
would lay orphanhood upon us;

over us, arms arched in safety,
a canopy of chestnut, elm, beech,
mulberry, safe haven for solitary
travelers: no tigers or bears,
but no signposts either; before we

moved ahead oblivious, then hoisted
between us her four limbs, swung her
with the abandon of children
whose mother would never commit
the treason of abandonment;

so that she hid her knowing pain in
chuckles as her cheap print skirt
rucked up, flashing on my 12-year-old sight
astonishing yellow camiknickers;

then tiring stopped to rest
as we rushed on, on the stolen
steps of night thieves
creeping away through the shades
of the dying afternoon.

# Communal Living

When we were young and immortal
what would we have said,
if an angel had come down
to our shack in Oregon's green
hills, as we warmed ourselves
beside the woodstove in a dark
soot-laden dawn, waiting for
Enid to make a pot of oatmeal,
Wayne to chop more wood;

if she waded her way among the piles
of duffel bags, the psychedelic
watercolors, the cans of Bugler,
packs of Camels with rising suns,
waves of color and stars drawn on,
found us in overalls and hiking boots,
our long cotton paisley skirts,
hair down past the waist, our manes
blowing in the smoky early morning
as we rolled our first cigarettes
or weed, maybe someone put on The Band,
Jackie Lomax or Fresh Cream.

She would furl her wings, point and
say — you, dead at 23, a suicide; you,
medical school; you, a life of loss and
unemployment; you, a mother, activist
in Vermont; you, filmmaker in Russia;
you, one year of law school, one son,
then dead at 40, an unnamed virus.
Would we have tilted back our
uncombed heads and laughed?

MICHAEL LIEBERMAN

# On the Anniversary of My Father's Death

I scoop up fine sand with the plastic shovel
of a small boy, funneling it over you
in pinions. Grasp her tail feathers, father,
rise with the heat. Surge through the dark veins
to their last branchings. Forget Helbros watches.

Roll the desk top down, leave Pittsburgh,
its gritty window sills. Let your silver body
rise up so I can feel the withered muscles
of your back. Make love to the show girl
from Las Vegas you have dreamed of.

Dailiness sucked your large brightness to a dry
socket. Stretch yourself out on the flatness
of the world — let this tribute draw the terror
from you. Seventeen years too late, I am arriving
indecently with the covered dish I owe you.

How can I find you, not below the proper Jewish
headstone in the high Reform cemetery, but where
you pitch and yawl, longing to trim your body
Out of turbulence, unless I release myself
from the stubble to a dry dispersing wind?

# Regret

One day you will slip into an airport,
stride past the phones, jingling your change,
and toss your hanging case into a cab.
You will feel only the slightest twinge
as you realize that I live in the city —
in good health, but old and somewhat frail —
that you will see me alive
perhaps a dozen times more,
and then only in orchestrated visits.
You will give a small shudder of regret
and move on. On that day you
will have learned what I have taught you.

MICHAEL LIEBERMAN

# Los Olivos

*for Ron Serrano (1941–1964)*

The olive trees grow silently in patches on the shoulders
of this town with its roll of ochre and California oak.
The palms droop over the earth as if to scoop up the air
which hesitates and stammers as it rises. The tongue
of the afternoon is too parched to speak. Suddenly my wife
mentions you, and I realize they should have buried you here
in the dry land, on top of a small mesa as if it were
an altar to offer up your presence above the fields and ranches
where irrigation matters, where your knowledge
of flow and turbulence would count for something.
What has been spoken under the rose between you two
over thirty years is unclear. What is unspoken between us
is that I married the woman you should have married,
fathered the children you should have fathered.
It is I who watch the hawks dizzy themselves
as if their calculated drift upward could bring rain
to this land beyond the Coastal Range.
I do not believe you soar with those hawks — or anywhere —
nor do you rest. But evanescent gods may watch over you
who are now mostly the water you dreamed of.
Surely if there is grace, they would bestow it
on a giver of water. They would come forward
to bless your graphs and equations.
I see the crimson bougainvillea in aneurysmal bursts
along the railroad and think of the explosion in your skull
and how simple mechanical failure has left me
to honor you as you had honored me in your choosing.

# potter

*for Emma, with Paget's disease of the breast*

took
two snowdrops to fall off the world
and land on the autumn of our damp sheets
before you could walk all night forever, until morning, and find our
    safehouse
with their white-silk injuries pressed carefully to your breast.
took
two summers before you'd return
to this harbourtown where we have found love like hurt
with driftwood and secrets to burn down in moonlight
and in their meagre heat, somehow charm dark earth
into circles
convinced of the reasons for our innocence.
once, it's true, we may have held out
against feint powderburns of spring, but they would have found us
and we will be found out
by robbingmen from the city who have come to harm us
unfolding our loveletters' scented origami
and scattering them through the garden.
don't fall, when all we can do now is lie in slow motion
listening to waves whisper up against the pier, and windmills
west of us, spin dark clouds into silence.
you promised, and you have come back from the world
with coloured stones and stories of winters
circling winter, our lady of the sewers and her children
lost beneath cardboard sails that ripple
on garbage oceans, so poor they must sell driftwood like secrets
burnt down from the northernmost of storms.
don't fall.
just fold your favourite dress across our two loves colliding,
its white-silk, even in moonlight, is bloodstained at the nipple.
but we will ignore these warnings and won't be frightened anymore,
even when they find us here, and we must hand over

all our coloured stones and sadnesses; we will keep these snowdrops
   hidden.
we will stay in love forever, until morning.

AUDREY SHAFER

# Monday Morning

In the prelight
A heavy sound from upstairs
I turn from the front door
   to investigate.

My three-year-old son stands
         naked
   in the soft penumbra of dimmed hallway light
Clutching his favorite blanket
   picture book and well-rubbed panther
      to his chest.
His toes curl on the wooden floor.

I am dressed and beepered —
No snuggling in the warm waterbed this morning
   floating back to sleep till sunlight wakens.
Instead, we hug.
I kiss
      his thin neck.
I feel his small breaths.

His bedroom door stands closed,
   heavy in shadows.

At the operating suite,
The residents still at lecture
The patient not yet here,
I enjoy the rote motions —
   follow the green snake tubing to the ceiling
   barbotage dissolving drugs into syringes
   snap open the laryngoscope.

Around me all is bright   pristine   ordered
Primed.
Sterile instruments attend in precise, metallic rows.

I try to recall his just-awakened warmth
   in that brief moment
      before

The patient arrives
Naked under hospital issue
Ready to sleep.

# The Bass

Because I was 37 and he was 10
I was presumed and of course
to know everything important

plus
how to take the fish off the hook.
I'd been told largemouth

and striped bass
both      either
waited for us below

the still crystal of the lake
I had no expectation though
of actually catching a fish

when somehow we did
After we hauled it heavily
in over the gunwales

like a glittering glory
no way was I about to touch
that wide mouth, those razor fins

gills, those sparkling cold-blooded
scales
until all spasm stopped

To this day my son
may think the way
to take a fish off the hook

is to place it, hook still intact
in the bottom of the boat
place a paddle over the fish

and keep your foot gently but steadfastly
on the paddle on the fish
After the flailing and flopping

I managed with something like
experience to get the hook out
Then as morning broke over us

we made our slow electric way
back to the boathouse
That fish won for us

a trophy
which I keep here on my desk
to remind me of that morning and of

how unexpected the end may be
how hungry
how shining

# Rosemary

6 A.M. All over the world
people are sleeping in shifts.
Rosemary is my waitress.

Not only is she beautiful
she brings me food and herbs
from the stores of her pantry.

From the looks of her
the legs are the last to go.
To, fro, she has a most remarkable walk

anatomy-proud, pendulum-perfect.
Does she have children
a husband        asleep

off somewhere in this remote new day?
It's ill advised to ask such questions
yet they're what I'd like to know

after an evening
in the arms of the Sheraton.
Last names are never put

on name tags now
have you noticed?
They could be used as proof.

Besides
a last name is too intimate.
A name tag like *Rosemary*

is properly civil
opaque as a servant.
I tell her my name is John.

There is a buffet
which I approach under the gaze
of a Jack O'Lantern

set up against those
who would take too much bacon.
I choose freely, with the magical joy

of hunger, taking some extra bacon
and stroll back with my plate.
There is so much

I'd like to have Rosemary tell me
but she pirouettes
constantly, table to table

pouring coffee,
resetting the places
for the other nameless

numb nightcrawlers
descended from
their Posturized beds

into the subdued light
of this morning place.
The businessmen

are reading the grim papers,
wiping their mouths, leaving,
a gnaw now in their upper abdomens.

My fourth cup of coffee
is strong, doing
its intravenous work.

Suddenly I realize that Rosemary and I
are alone in this place.
She sits herself down

at a table across the room
to have her own quick breakfast.
The sun is coming in through her hair.

I want to call her over, say
*Rosemary, sit down*
then read her this poem.

But there is no such thing
as a simple pleasure.
I have the feeling she knows

# Talking to the Family

My white coat waits in the corner
like a father.
I will wear it to meet the sister
in her white shoes and organza dress
in the live of winter,

the milkless husband
holding the baby.

I will tell them.

They will put it together
and take it apart.
Their voices will buzz.
The cut ends of their nerves
will curl.

I will take off the coat,
drive home,
and replace the light bulb in the hall.

MARC J. STRAUS

# What I Heard on the Radio Today

Horowitz debuted a Schumann piece
in 1928. This new recording
is acoustically precise, with
a persistent cough from the audience,

loud, in two parts, both exhaled sounds,
(B-flat, then C-sharp) the second
higher and more forceful. It sounds like
a man's cough, a mature man,

in his 40s or 50s. You can tell these things
just as you can guess gender and age
from a voice on the phone. This man coughing,
not covering his mouth, no handkerchief muffle,

may have served in World War I. He would have been
of moderate rank, a sergeant in charge
of a platoon. He took orders
and gave orders. He may have worked

in an insurance firm, and sold policies
to pensioners. Now V.P.
and three kids in school, life was bright.
Coolidge was President. He had 42,000 dollars

in assorted stocks. And, Horowitz,
Horowitz was a skinny Jew from Russia
who could play piano, but Jews
were good at things like that. Russia

and Poland knew how to treat their Jews.
And, here at Carnegie Hall, at 4 dollars
a ticket, he played Schumann
with such intended panache. The cough

continued as the concert went on.
I know that cough. I've heard it
listening to many lungs
on TB wards. It has its own pattern

and tone. His cough worsened in a year
when the market crashed. His breath
became more shallow. His stocks
were worthless. His daughter married a Jew.

Late, much too late, he'd be moved to
a sanitarium and die in '32.
There remains a recording of him
that I heard on the radio today.

# Before the Brain Surgery

We'd moved out. You'd stayed behind alone
to rid the vacant room of our last traces.
It grew dark. The light switch wouldn't work.
Your limbs froze in the usual paresis;
your throat closed inches from the telephone.

That, of course, was the dark stranger's cue
and probably the moment when you cried
out, dreaming. It was an owlish sound,
one I'd never heard you make, that died
into a snore, then breath. How unlike you,

to call out in your sleep! I kicked your thigh.
Next morning, over coffee, you recalled
the room, the dark, the stranger and your scream.
You kicked me? I must say, dear, I'm appalled.
Whenever you have nightmares, don't I try

to ease you out of them with loving arms?
Quite true. And, often, it's from the same room
where lights malfunction, strangers come, and screams
get stuck in throats — generic signs of doom
that never quite portend specific harm.

Not like your nightmare. I already knew
the shadows gathering inside the dome,
me lying in the darkness outside you,
the glinting blade, you lying there alone.
The stranger. Darling, it's my nightmare, too.

It spans insomnia, and restless sleep,
a bridge that neither one of us can cross.
Next time let's meet halfway, where the bed sags,
both sleep and wakefulness a total loss,
suspended over something swift and deep.

# The Portugal Laurel

At times I fear,
after decades of doctoring,
of stashing tears in the pockets
of a long white coat,

my soul has turned to salt.

Take for example, the Portugal Laurel.
It has graced the patio for thirty-five years,
grown up with the family, seen sorrows, joys.
It has provided shade and beauty —
following a morning rain, it sparkles
in the afternoon sun, a million pieces
of dark green crystal, carnelian stems.
And, many a mid-night, its branches
have hid the ashes of a sleepless cigar.
But now, children gone, the patio is a ruin.
The landscape architect proclaims,
"We need to open this space, it has to go."

So yesterday I took the laurel down,
not the slightest hesitation. At the start,
I was occupied by technical matters — how to
bring down a robust laurel safely,
how to dispose of it. Never mind the details,
but, you know, I had to use a chain saw —
the trunk was twelve inches at the base.
In an hour and a half it was gone, all except
the weeping stump, an injured friend seeking
an explanation. Only then — only when
confronted by that personal void —
did I feel a single shiver of sadness.

See what I mean?

And today? Well, today
I have this pale blue numbness,
which I know by tomorrow
will be gone.

JOHN WRIGHT

# Transfiguration

Underpants
lying limp, shapeless
on the bathroom floor

Shoes scattered
by ones and twos
throughout the house

Yesterday's newspaper
in disarray
over the library rug

Earrings and watch,
keys and glasses
chronically mislaid

These common objects
once grew Dragon size,
inflamed my senses

But through a gradual
*Transfiguration*
they have become

Small and comforting
reminders of you,
who from the beginning

Accepted
with minimal complaints
my psoriatic scales

And all other less
genetically programmed
errors.

# "in ways that helped them see"

The transmission of knowledge from teacher to student, how it occurs, under what circumstances, as well as the relationship between the two, is the subject of poems which celebrate the learning process. While medical school and hospital are the settings for most of the works herein collected, others situate the learning experience in less likely locations, such as a greenhouse or a high school laboratory. Teachers are not always as one would expect them to be. Lessons are not always learned from textbooks. Ultimately, it is the nature of the truth passed on which is of account.

In "On Dutch's Death" the unexpected news of the passing of a favorite teacher brings a rush of memories to mind for Robert Coles, who recalls vividly the most valuable lesson taught him by his mentor: the fine art of *seeing* a patient, the crucial element in the healing connection. Dutch provided a model of empathy in the physician-patient relationship, directing others "in ways that helped them see." David Moolten fondly remembers another teacher in "Bio 7." The lessons taught by Mr. Gordon equip a boy with the confidence needed to absorb the more challenging lessons to come. The same poet encountered one of those challenging lessons when he said goodbye to Richie Savalo in "Motorcycle Ward." At one level he learned to depend on "slow-witted cars" instead of motorcycles. At a deeper level, he discovered "a terrible narration / In the thrumming cylinders of my heart."

While medicine today benefits from an unprecedented development of knowledge and the means to acquire it, we are often reminded of a time when facts were fewer and their acquisition came at great cost. With "In the Theatre" Dannie Abse records a lesson from the past never to be forgotten. Based on a true incident witnessed by the poet's father, the poem describes an early operation to remove a brain tumor. The crude hit-or-miss technique of the surgeon results in the destruction of healthy brain tissue. From the core of his being, the partially anesthetized patient sounds a protest against the destruction of his soul.

And where do we find the soul? Rafael Campo considers the study of the human body "terrible" until he discovers the beauty of its "sleek interior." In "What the Body Told" he learns that the soul is "each nameless cell contributing its needs." Anatomy and physiology reveal truths which lead to a wide awareness of the unity of life. D. A. Feinfeld's "The Wound Man," speaking from a sixteenth-century first-aid chart, tells us ironically that no one has provided for *his* soul. While exhibiting a variety of wounds likely to occur during warfare, the dispassionate figure depicted in the drawing would like to — but cannot — express a deep wound of the soul. An unrecognized component of his makeup are the tears which distinguish his humanity.

Equally tearless, though presenting real skin and organs to the scalpel-wielding student, the cadavers in Dannie Abse's "Carnal Knowledge" and Jack Coulehan's "Anatomy Lesson" provide a further dimension. They retain sufficient spiritual identity to instill a sense of culpability in those who violate them and to make the dissection somewhat less than casual. In James Foy's "Autopsy" the poet learns of the consonance which exists between the human and the natural worlds, the changing seasons of which are reflected in the body's essential structure.

The young doctor in Eric Dyer's "Painting the Nude" instructs his teacher in viewing the inert form of an intubated patient from the perspective of an artist painting a natural object. He would like to infuse the figure with the warm colors of a bright day, rather than "blood red" and "bilious mixtures." Similarly, in "Venipuncture" John Graham-Pole's intern expresses a desire for a different reality. His feelings of frustration and ineptitude reveal that the acquisition of skills is not without cost; it takes its toll on the young doctor as well as on the patient.

Facts of the more conventional kind are to be learned in Coulehan's "The Rule of Thirds." The "rule" is the law of averages, which is written in "the language of the body / in its genes." Despite the many lessons learned and the accumulation of numberless facts, questions remain that baffle the mature professional. As Marc J. Straus describes in "The Log of Pi," "they always ask the question / I never knew." The mature physician in Arthur Ginsberg's "Line Drive" learns a valuable lesson from ballplayers in a schoolyard. Witnessing an accident during a game, he observes the love and concern with which the team members bolster the injured player. As a result of this experience, he knows he must go back to the hospital to lend the warmth of his touch to a dying patient.

After all the classes have been taken and all the examinations passed, the careers begin. In the Commencement poem "*Gaudeamus Igitur*: A Valediction," John Stone previews for the graduates the joys and disappointments of life in the profession of medicine. The day begins on a triumphant note of joy. Whatever the future holds, what matters most is love and the human spirit which it nourishes. The mature physician entreats the young graduates to seek answers in the customary places but not to ignore the unexpected, "For Mozart can heal and no one knows where he is buried." Reflecting generally on the arts and their value in the lives of the emerging doctors, Stone instructs them: "For there will be the arts / and some will call them / soft data / Whereas in fact they are the hard data / by which our lives are lived."

# Carnal Knowledge

### 1

You, student, whistling those elusive bits
of Schubert when phut, phut, phut, throbbed the sky
of London. Listen: the servo-engine cut
and the silence was not the desired silence
between two movements of music. Then
Finale, the Aldwych echo of crunch
and the urgent ambulances loaded
with the fresh dead. You, young, whistled again,
entered King's, climbed the stone-murky steps
to the high and brilliant Dissecting Room
where nameless others, naked on the slabs,
reclined in disgraceful silences — twenty
amazing sculptures waiting to be vandalized.

### 2

You, corpse, I pried into your bloodless meat
without the morbid curiousity of Vesalius,
did not care that the great Galen was wrong,
Avicenna mistaken, that they had described
the approximate structure of pigs and monkeys
rather than the human body. With scalpel
I dug deep into your stale formaldehyde
unaware of Pope Boniface's decree
but, as instructed, violated you —
the reek of you in my eyes, my nostrils,
clothes, in the kisses of my girlfriends.
You, anonymous. Who were you, mister?
Your thin mouth could not reply, "Absent, sir,"
or utter the inquisitionary rage.

Your neck exposed, muscles, nerves, vessels,
a mere coloured plate in some anatomy book;
your right hand, too, dissected, never belonged,
it seemed, to somebody once shockingly alive,

never held, surely, another hand in greeting
or tenderness, never clenched a fist in anger,
never took up a pen to sign an authentic name.
   You, dead man, Thing, each day, each week,
each month, you, slowly decreasing Thing,
visibly losing Divine proportions,
you residue, mere trunk of a man's body,
you, X, legless, armless, headless Thing
that I dissected so casually.
   Then went downstairs to drink wartime coffee.


3

When the hospital priest, Father Jerome,
remarked, "The Devil made the lower parts
of a man's body, God the upper,"
I said, "Father, it's the other way round."
So, the anatomy course over, Jerome,
thanatologist, did not invite me
to the Special Service for the Twenty Dead,
did not say to me, "Come for the relatives' sake."
(Surprise, surprise, that they had relatives,
those lifeless-size, innominate creatures.)

Other students accepted, joined in the fake chanting,
organ solemnity, cobwebbed theatre.
And that's all it would have been,
a ceremony propitious and routine,
an obligation forgotten soon enough
had not the strict priest with premeditated rage
called out the Register of the Twenty Dead —
each noncephalic carcass gloatingly identified
with a local habitation and a name
till one by one, made culpable, the students cried.


4

I did not learn the name of my intimate,
the twentieth sculpture, the one next to the door.

No matter. Now all these years later
I know those twenty sculptures were but one,
the same one duplicated. You.
I hear not Father Jerome but St. Jerome cry,
"No, John will be John, Mary will be Mary,"
as if the dead would have ears to hear
the Register on Judgment Day.
    Look, on gravestones many names.
There should be one only. Yours.
No, not even one since you have no name.
In the newspapers' memorial columns
many names. A joke.
On the canvases of masterpieces
the same figure always in disguise. Yours.
Even in the portraits of the old anchorite
fingering a dry skull you are half concealed
lest onlookers should turn away blinded.
In certain music, too, with its sound of loss,
in that Schubert Quintet, for instance,
you are there in the Adagio,
playing the third cello that cannot be heard.
    You are there and there and there, nameless,
and here I am, older by far and nearer,
perplexed, trying to recall what you looked like
before I dissected your face — you, threat,
molesting presence, and I in a white coat
your enemy, in a purple one, your nuncio,
writing this while a winter twig, not you,
scrapes, scrapes the windowpane.

DANNIE ABSE

# In the Theatre

(A true incident)
*Only a local anaesthetic was given because of the blood pressure
problem. The patient, thus, was fully awake throughout the
operation. But in those days — in 1938, in Cardiff, where I
was Lambert Rogers' dresser — they could not locate a brain
tumour with precision. Too much normal brain tissue was
destroyed as the surgeon crudely searched for it, before he felt
the resistance of it . . . all somewhat hit and miss. One
operation I shall never forget. . . .* (Dr. Wilfred Abse)

Sister saying — "Soon you'll be back in the ward,"
sister thinking — "Only two more on the list,"
the patient saying — "Thank you, I feel fine";
small voices, small lies, nothing untoward,
though, soon, he would blink again and again
because of the fingers of Lambert Rogers,
rash as a blind man's, inside his soft brain.

If items of horror can make a man laugh
then laugh at this: one hour later, the growth
still undiscovered, ticking its own wild time;
more brain mashed because of the probe's Braille path;
Lambert Rogers desperate, fingering still;
his dresser thinking, "Christ! Two more on the list,
a cisternal puncture and a neural cyst."

Then, suddenly, the cracked record in the brain,
a ventriloquist voice that cried, "You sod,
leave my soul alone, leave my soul alone" —
the patient's dummy lips moving to that refrain,
the patient's eyes too wide. And, shocked,
Lambert Rogers drawing out the probe
with nurses, students, sister, petrified.

"Leave my soul alone, leave my soul alone,"
that voice so arctic and that cry so odd
had nowhere else to go — till the antique
gramophone wound down and the words began

to blur and slow, " . . . leave . . . my . . . soul . . . alone . . ."
to cease at last when something other died.
And silence matched the silence under snow.

# The Origin of Music

When I was a medical student
I stole two femurs of a baby
from The Pathology Specimen Room.
Now I keep them in my pocket,
the right femur and the left femur.
Like a boy scout, I'm prepared.
For what can one say to a neighbour
when his wife dies? "Sorry"?
Or when a friend's sweet child
suffers leukaemia? "Condolences"?
No, if I should meet either friend
or stricken neighbour in the street
and he should tell me, whisper to me,
his woeful, intimate news,
wordless I take the two small femurs
from out of my pocket sadly
and play them like castanets.

# What the Body Told

Not long ago, I studied medicine.
It was terrible, what the body told.
I'd look inside another person's mouth,
And see the desolation of the world.
I'd see his genitals and think of sin.

Because my body speaks the stranger's language,
I've never understood those nods and stares.
My parents held me in their arms, and still
I think I've disappointed them; they care,
They stare and nod, they make their pilgrimage

To somewhere distant in my heart, they cry.
I look inside their other-person's mouths
And see the sleek interior of souls.
It's warm and red in there — like love, with teeth.
I've studied medicine until I cried ·

All night. Through certain books, a truth unfolds.
Anatomy and physiology,
The tiny sensing organs of the tongue —
Each nameless cell contributing its needs.
It was fabulous, what the body told.

ROBERT COLES

# On Dutch's Death

*In memory of A. O. L.*

The doctor's face on a December day —
Dutch died, the papers say.
I learned later,
Returning to the city where he taught me
How to listen,
Help build up another's ego
By digging into my own;
How to speak
When a moment presses with all its might
On ears kept warm by the old pump
Whose workings he knew so well —
The years at the General with bodies
Before the mind made its summons.
All morning with rich analysands,
All afternoon with poor drunks
Who came to a clinic he ran.
We ran, too — eager for his "pearls."
(I started hearing the word in medical school;
I remembered how easily my mother wore them,
How hard they came to us.)

For him psychoanalysis was not the high of heady abstractions;
Rather, to keep steady,
Keep trucking
Through the fog, the crooked paths
Which lead to walls the ancient Chinese would admire —
Until a doctor's words seem late,
Already heard by the patient.
He taught that a mirror
Need not be a fawning or dread double
But, when held at the right angle
To the sun of alert study,
A means of exposure and cautery:
"Warm things up," he once said,
"Then be prepared to take the heat."

Late in life he kept the fires going.
A wise beauty lasted
Until the very end,
So they said who had gotten in dutch,
Who had gone to see Dutch,
Who loved him as a Dutch uncle
As well as a savvy alienist,
Never a stranger to those he "saw"
In ways that helped them see.

JACK COULEHAN

# Anatomy Lesson

When I move your body
from its storage drawer,
I brush my knuckles,
Ernest, on your three-days
growth of beard. Checks,
wet with formaldehyde,
prickle with cactus.
My eyes burn and blink
as if a wind of sand
blew through the room.

Bless me, Ernest,
for I cut your skin
to learn positions
and connections
of your parts — caves,
canyons, fissures, faults,
all of you. Show me.
Show me your flowers,
your minerals, the oil
of your spleen.

Do not mistake these tears.
These tears are not
for your bad luck
nor my indenture here,
but for all offenses
to the heart — yours, mine —
for the violence
of abomination.
Think of my tears as rain
staining your canyon walls,
filling your stream,
touching the blossoms.

# The Rule of Thirds

*Third, third, third* — the rule I learned
about the stories of the ill.

A third get well — joints begin to move,
pain improves, depression's dull

embrace is eased. The villain leaves
without a trace and no one knows

the hero's name — doctor
or the patient, science or the grace.

A third grow crippled in the pain
of joints gone stone, their minds decline,

the villain takes the loot no matter what
your dour professor does, or you —

in the arrogance of youth — might try.
*We learn by progress in our minds.*

A third remain the same. They take
the villain in, they harbor him

until his tale is theirs and theirs is his.
They visualize their bodies with his eyes.

Our rule of thirds was not as kind
as love's compassion is,

nor as thunderous as an essay
on machines, but it spoke

the language of the body
in its genes.

ERIC DYER

# Painting the Nude

His morning posture is sketched naked,
unresponsive under sheets and brushed
by tracheostomy and nasogastric tubes,
oh God, by Swan-Ganz catheter and Foley.

Teacher, could I begin our class today
with a clean, white, uncomplicated canvas
instead of this cracked portrait
streaked with yesterday's caprice?

May I ask for just one day strong
in the warms of pink and yellow?
You know how fussy I am about skin tones
and adjusting the flow of genitalia so so.

May this palette be spared today
from blood red and cyan blue;
no greens or browns either, please,
or bilious mixtures of the two.

And may I have no black at all
to distract from the strokes of light
infusing this splattered smock I wear
and breaking at last from his opening eyes.

D. A. FEINFELD

# The Wound Man

*A 16th-century first-aid chart showing the location*
*and nature of wounds occurring during war.*

Stabbed, clubbed, and slashed, I stand;
a dozen shafts splay from my body

as flashes from a lantern,
but my burning gives no light.

Sebastian, shot only with arrows,
saw paradise beyond his pain;

I stand with shocked flesh forever
staring through the eyes of my wounds,

my sight bounded by dagger-hafts
and the shadows of club and hatchet.

For your instruction, I remain
ever erect and ever silent,

allowed not even the grace
of a cry, grimace, or clenched jaw.

The drops brightening on my face
are but blood. I am granted no tears.

JAMES L. FOY

# Autopsy

*for Richard Selzer*

It comes as a surprise once more
When the abdominal cavity is opened
And there is discovered a Summer
Of waving grass under a seamless sky
Overwhelming in clarity and something
Like happiness. There is the usual
commotion of bees and small insects
Fumbling the flowers, birdsong also
And the bright sheen on the viscera
Is the sun at its zenith.

Deep in the pelvis a wind shakes
The leaving trees, here and there
Chrysanthemums are in bloom among
The drillings of the last cicadas.
Autumn twilight comes slowly with
A gradual chill. Mounds of raked
Leaves are burning and raising
Towers of smoke, which stand up
Through the amber light. Fires
Will smolder until moonrise.

Upon opening the chest the lungs
Emerge, a Winter landscape of snow
Strewn fields marked by a black
Calligraphy of twiggy bushes and
Leafless vines. An ancestor crow
With blue-black wings descends
On a branch but utters no cry.
Listless eyes survey emptiness.
The sun is concealed somewhere,
It is biding time.

Only when the great vessels are
Exposed and severed, and the four
Chambered heart is laid open to

Inspection, does Spring appear
In glory and abundance. First
seen are the cherry blossoms,
Magnolia and apple; followed
In steady vernal sequence by
Tulip, azalea, iris, and finally
The peony in its ecstasy.

Birds are now everywhere calling
And filling all space with their
Nervous disorder. It seems morning
Survives the livelong day. Rooted
Things dig down and assert themselves
In predictable systole and diastole
With a unison giving and taking
Of the breath in a living equinox,
A moment of renewal at the apex
Of the naked heart.

At the end it is reassuring to note
That the brain, the last sector
To be examined, holds within some
Shattered echo of each season.
Certainly it is the anatomy
Of rhythm, time and remembrance.
But most of all it mirrors
The skies of April: scudding clouds,
Birds on the wing, sunshine after
Rain, a petal or two.

# Line Drive

I had come from a dying man's room.
What I said, addressed the cancer
eroding his brain, how his right side
would become limp, he would slowly
slip into a coma. And, I pointed out
the silver shadow on black film from
the foot of his bed, staying at
bed's length from him and his widow-to-be.
And, I said too little, too quickly
for the quivering ears and lips
where death was digging in, and,
I forgot to touch or be touched.

On the way home, I passed a schoolyard.
It was a fine day, the light scattered
in shafts on the dark brown earth
of the baseball diamond. Clover
grew in clumps by the side of the field,
white tendrils pulling in the bees.
I stood outside the chainlink fence
watching the game in progress. Everything
was shouting, *Hallelujah, alive! alive!*
A mother cat cuffed her kittens into line,
taught them to balance on the schoolyard big-toy
and old retreads hooked one to another,
swaying gently in the breeze. I jumped the fence
to get closer to the game when the batter
hit a line drive into the pitcher's stomach.

He dropped like a stone but was, in moments,
surrounded by Billy and Peter and Rob and
the first baseman holding his head, his sobbing,
coaxing him to breathe, *you'll live, it will be o.k.*
I knew I must go back to the man
dying in white linen and say nothing more
than the warmth of my hands in his.

# Venipuncture

In the callows of my intern year of
sixty-seven, I kept the company of
big leukemia men, often so unstickable
I shrank from them; stuck so often
without issue but blasphemy of
tears leaking from the both of us.

I pinioned once a nameless tributary vein,
harnessed thick of shoulder, elbow,
supinated wrist at outermost rotation,
forcing a twist to the neck cords as
blue line on ulnar pulp bulged,
skittered squeamish, coy around my darts

until the time the hematoma sprang
screaming its livid tracer on the passes
of ineptitude, pricked me to sacrilege:
he'll die anyway (they all did then),
the blasphemy of blame: God why this
tiny vessel in this gargantuan frame?

# Motorcycle Ward

I can't say much about Richie Savalo
A boy scraped out from under an eighteen-wheeler
Except that he owned a Harley 650
And at sixteen I thought I couldn't live
Without one. I can't say I knew him
Beyond a ride or two and the day I joined
The other seniors who paraded to say goodbye
On the trauma floor. A surgeon —
Who tried to convince us that we didn't need
All that verb from a stoplight,
All that mind-altering power and open air
Like skinnydipping or TV made wild
And electric without the glass — proclaimed it
The motorcycle ward. We saw everything:
The long halls, the nurses passing sadly,
Each room identical, patients already
Partly embalmed in their casts. When we looked
They squinted back as though in some chrome glare
Beneath the syllabic drips of IVs —
That is, if they could surface through the morphine.
We found Richie, who they never quite
Pieced together with pins and prayer.
The day made me as green as when I first
Tried cigarettes. After that there would be
No bike, just a long line of slow-witted cars.
I can't say other effects were lasting
Although I did have nightmares for a while,
Not precisely about Richie or motorcycles,
The darkness more visceral than cinematic,
Which was perhaps merely the closeness
To the dead that comes with fear,
A sleeping empathy. There was only
The hair-trigger escape, the hurtling
Upwards or away from whatever bore down
On me until I felt that torque
Which the moment of waking brings

And over the dark terrain of the bedclothes,
I had outrun everything but a strange
Realization of luck and a terrible narration
In the thrumming cylinders of my heart.

# Bio 7

The year of their ultimate squalor,
Of my father's gum-chewing brunette
With the legs and the split quartz gray eyes,
Of my mother's overall violence, her premature
And less than sentimental eulogies for him,
Was the year of their separation.
It was also the year of the bad grades,
Of Bio 7, pithing frogs, and shucking
The durable exoskeleton of crayfish.
It was the year of Mr. Gordon,
Who pioneered us through each prosection
And made clear the vital and multitiered truths
Beneath all the slaughter. Many days
He kept me after, preaching mitosis
From the ancient slides, forcing me
To stare cross-eyed into microscopes
Until it made sense, telling me I hadn't
Fooled him, that he knew what was going on,
That I was bright, and that I could cry
If I had to. I remember how excited he became
Over prophase, when the invisible
DNA one assumed on faith, like heaven
Or honesty, thickened to jelly,
And metaphase where under oil immersion
I actually saw the chromosomes paired
And lined up like intimate dancers
Or just plain lovers. And having seen
Endless acres of local prime cattle,
All that roan poundage back-crossed
To perfection, I conceived easily
Of the double helix and Mendel's peas.
Even with my blank stare and C−,
That we were just versions of our parents
Scrambled like cryptograms, seemed straightforward —
No rustic doctrine that genetics
Are the only code we're guaranteed to live by.

Perhaps beyond the empirical dice-throws,
The inexorable certainty of the whole affair
Clicked for me too, a process more stuck-switch
Than blind urge, the cells all machine-like
Precision, dividing and pressing on without
Passion or need. I remember the night
My parents explained, how I stared at them —
Him with my eyes, her with my jet-black hair —
Still trying to comprehend the point
They'd made, even as the cutting had begun.

# *Gaudeamus Igitur*: A Valediction

For this is the day of joy
    which has been fourteen hundred and sixty days in coming
For today in the breathing name of Brahms
    and the cat of Christopher Smart
    through the unbroken line of language and all the nouns
    stored in the angular gyrus
    today is a commencing
For this is the day you know too little
    against the day when you will know too much
For you will be invincible
    and vulnerable in the same breath
    which is the breath of your patients
For their breath is our breathing and our reason
For the patient will know the answer
    and you will ask him
    ask her
For the family may know the answer
For there may be no answer
    and you will know too little again
    or there *will* be an answer and you will know too much forever
For you will look smart and feel ignorant
    and the patient will not know which day it is for you
    and you will pretend to be smart out of ignorance
For you must fear ignorance more than cyanosis
For whole days will move in the direction of rain
For you will cry and there will be no one to talk to
    or no one but yourself
For you will be lonely
For you will be alone
For there is a difference
For there is no seriousness like joy
For there is no joy like seriousness
For the days will run together in gallops and the years
    go by as fast as the speed of thought
    which is faster than the speed of light

or Superman
or Superwoman
For you will not be Superman
For you will not be Superwoman
For you will not be Solomon
      but you will be asked the question nevertheless
For after you learn what to do, how and when to do it
      the question will be *whether*
For there will be addictions: whiskey, tobacco, love
For they will be difficult to cure
For you yourself will pass the kidney stone of pain
      and be joyful
For this is the end of examinations
For this is the beginning of testing
For Death will give the final examination
      and everyone will pass
For the sun is always right on time
      and even that may be reason for a kind of joy
For there are all kinds of
      all degrees of joy
For love is the highest joy
For which reason the best hospital is a house of joy
      even with rooms of pain and loss
      exits of misunderstanding
For there is the mortar of faith
For it helps to believe
For Mozart can heal and no one knows where he is buried
For penicillin can heal
      and the word
      and the knife
For the placebo will work and you will think you know why
For the placebo will have side effects and you will know you do not
      know why
For none of these may heal
For joy is nothing if not mysterious
For your patients will test you for spleen
      and for the four humors
For they will know the answer
For they have the disease

For disease will peer up over the hedge
       of health, with only its eyes showing
For the T waves will be peaked and you will not know why
For there will be computers
For there will be hard data and they will be hard to understand
For the trivial will trap you and the important escape you
For the Committee will be unable to resolve the question
For there will be the arts
       and some will call them
       soft data
       whereas in fact they are the hard data
       by which our lives are lived
For everyone comes to the arts too late
For you can be trained to listen only for the oboe
       out of the whole orchestra
For you may need to strain to hear the voice of the patient
       in the thin reed of his crying
For you will learn to see most acutely out of
       the corner of your eye
       to hear best with your inner ear
For there are late signs and early signs
For the patient's story will come to you
       like hunger, like thirst
For you will know the answer
       like second nature, like first
For the patient will live
       and you will try to understand
For you will be amazed
       or the patient will not live
       and you will try to understand
For you will be baffled
For you will try to explain both, either, to the family
For there will be laying on of hands
       and the letting go
For love is what death would always intend if it had the choice
For the fever will drop, the bone remold itself along
       its line of force
       the speech return
       the mind remember itself

For there will be days of joy
For there will be elevators of elation
    and you will walk triumphantly
    in purest joy
    along the halls of the hospital
    and say *Yes* to all the dark corners
    where no one is listening
For the heart will lead
For the head will explain
    but the final common pathway is the heart
    whatever kingdom may come
For what matters finally is how the human spirit is spent
For this is the day of joy
For this is the morning to rejoice
For this is the beginning
    Therefore, let us rejoice
    *Gaudeamus igitur.*

MARC J. STRAUS

# The Log of Pi

I remember the log of Pi, the battle
of Antietam, the insertion of the biceps, the action
of Adriamycin. Why? When's the last time
anyone asked these data? I've filled my head

with assorted facts, ordered and chronoed,
sorted and cataloged. Maybe a game show host
will choose me. I'll win stacks of money
answering questions about paramecia, Picasso's

pink period, the sequence of DNA, the dose
of 5FU. But no, they always ask the question
I never knew. They ask me over
and over again, every day. First

I pretend not to hear. Then I change
the subject. Then when pressed I say,
the answer floats on angel's lips
and is whispered in our ear just once.

# Neuroanatomy Summer

The even flow of neuronal pattern was visible
on the green screen, as tiny electrodes were placed
directly into portions of the cat's brain.

I was given the job of sectioning incremental portions
of the brain and measuring the cat's response,
reflexes, gait, etc., until it became

decerebrate, that is had no higher brain function
at all. Then the cat was rigid, fully stretched out
and unresponsive. What was remarkable the professor

said, was that I was able to take this cat
through twelve step-wise operations (surely the basis
of a paper) and keep the cat intact.

Later on I saw a man stretched out like that
and rigid with tubes in his nose and penis. Someone
more important than me was writing a paper, I thought.

# Scarlet Crown

I met a man my age running a greenhouse.
He pointed to the pots with pride, saying
they contained a thousand separate cacti.
Not much interest in these when I started,
he said. He pointed to the barbed bristles

(glochids), the bearing cushions (areoles),
and the names of many of the 200 genera:
Brain, Button, Cow-tongue, Hot-dog, Lace,
Coral, and Silver-ball. In my work,
I said, I'm burdened with such straight-

forward terms: lung cancer, lymphoma,
breast cancer, leukemia. I'd love
to switch to Pond-lily, Star,
or Scarlet Crown. Really, he said,
pointing to other plants, named

Hatchet, Devil, Dagger, Hook, and
Snake — or perhaps a diagnosis of this:
Rat-tail, White-chin, Wooly-torch,
or Dancing-bones.

# "... this was the music of our lives"

A citizen of the larger world beyond hospital, office, or home, the poet frequently focuses on matters more inclusive or general. His or her interest turns to issues of historical or social concern, to questions of local or even global relevance. Of note here is the extent to which the physician-poet brings a healing identity to bear on any subject. Often the medical sensibility, the medical perspective as it were, can be detected even in poems seeming to owe little or nothing to a medical source. On analysis one can establish a link. Consider the classic example — the work of John Keats, the Romantic poet. Numerous critics have failed traditionally to acknowledge the influence of Keats's medical background upon his verse. Current scholarship, though, views his exquisite sensitivity to human suffering as resulting in large measure from his formative years spent in training as a surgeon.

In his poem "Broken Silence" Louis Abbey provides a contemporary example of the same influence. Viewing an old snapshot that he took of a wartime incident he witnessed, Abbey considers the recent involvement of some neighbors in a car accident. Over in a moment, the mishap resulted in some superficial injuries to the victims, who are shortly comforted by well-wishers. In contrast, in a similarly brief time, the victims of the war are brutally annihilated. The only observers are soldiers. Except for the photographer, who alone is sensitive to the suffering endured by the likely-innocent victims, others stand impassively by.

John Graham-Pole personifies human suffering in "The Pain," where pain is viewed metaphorically as an acquaintance come for a visit. Once settled within the house, it never leaves. In "The Goddam Street" Robert Coles gives us a glimpse of a "cold rat-infested flat" where a loving mother strives through her warmth to create a barrier that preserves her children from the pain of poverty and discrimination.

A common scene on a highway takes on a new depth of meaning when viewed from the perspective of the physician in John Stone's "The Truck." Driving behind the vehicle named in the title, the poet finds his attention seized by the company name, PROGRESS CASKETS, prominently displayed. The name perplexes the physician, who cannot resolve the antithesis it suggests, at least not from a medical point of view.

The interior of an ordinary trolley car provides the setting for an extraordinary event in David Moolten's "Madame Butterfly" as a deranged passenger begins to scream incoherently. Conditioned to observe and to listen, the poet alone among the riders hears in her voice the note of grief and loss which reverberates in the heart of all humanity. The incident becomes for him an instance in which he grasps the hidden truth that "this was the music of our lives." Other passengers, schooled only in social decorum, merely look away. In the same poet's "Voyeur," an elderly man chooses not to look away, but, instead, watches "a woman disrobe in a window" and wonders if, indeed, he had ever truly loved his dead wife. When the woman he watches — she, too, is almost eighty — notices the voyeur, she "lets the curtains fall" but begins to reflect on her own life — "she too hears / Raucous music from her past."

A social statistic of statewide significance provides the subject of conversation for some simple folk, farmers in Richard Donze's "Vermont Has a High Suicide Rate." A local farmer-doctor in the area offers a simple explanation for the high figures. Another country doctor in H. J. Van Peenen's "Will Campbell Displays His Craniotribe" has an explanation of a different sort, one for a father whose child he is about to deliver. Placing his "craniotribe" on the kitchen table, he explains that the instrument is used to puncture an infant's head during the advanced stages of labor when the head is too large to pass through the birth canal and caesarian section is not available. The "craniotribe" is used to kill the baby in order to save the mother. A relic from an apparent barbaric past, the impressive device is most useful in getting the nervous father out of the room — and out of the doctor's way — in a hurry. Larger questions are pondered by H. J. Van Peenen in "Insulin Receptor" and by Michael Lieberman in "Prediction." The former poem considers the complexity of mutually dependent elements that make life possible, with the poet wondering "how we ever started / when an almost-nothing kills." In "Prediction" the poet views the end of the world from his physician's angle of vision, imagining the final moments to resemble "a division of skin or fascia at autopsy."

Robert Coles records life on distant shores in "Christmas, Belfast," where a nine-year-old girl whose parents dared to "intermarry" (one is Catholic, the other Protestant) reveals the chilling maturity that characterizes children raised in war-ravaged societies. She is pessimistic that the sectarian violence will cease, even as the opposing adults about her join together in prayer for peace at Christmas.

Further echoes of man's inhumanity to man resound in Norbert Hirschhorn's "Number Our Days," which is set against the background of the Holocaust. A woman who survived the terror lacks the strength to shake off the demons which pursued her into freedom. Her doctor-son is powerless to save her. Another woman to survive the flames that destroyed her childhood home and her family is the subject of Thomas Dorsett's "The Survivor." The long-dormant memories of the horror are awakened by the sound of a jet flying over the nursery home of her old age.

A somewhat insensitive son badgers his elderly parent on the necessity of taking vitamins in Ron Charach's "A Question of Vitamins." Assuming an authority he lacks, the son hammers away at the father until checked by the older man's unexpected retort, which concludes the work. All the vitamins in the world are ineffectual in the treatment of one ailment that has been part of human experience since Biblical times, at the very least. Indeed, despite centuries of progress in medicine, no new cures have been discovered. The malady is the subject of Jack Coulehan's "Lovesickness: A Medieval Text."

Figures out of the past populate such poems as Coulehan's "The Dynamizer and the Oscilloclast" and George Young's "Damien" and "The Miracle." Coulehan's work is a dramatic monologue delivered by a quack who attracts the sick with hocus-pocus devices. He has been so successful restoring people's hope with his dynamizer that now he must create an oscilloclast to cure them. Is he a consummate con artist? Or does he really believe he can help the sick?

"Damien" celebrates the Catholic missionary to the lepers at Molokai, he of the "priesthood of worms and rotting flesh." Powerless to cure the sick, he eventually becomes one of them. "The Miracle" celebrates a historical moment of great import for medicine. The poet identifies the inspiration for a Rembrandt masterpiece in an amazing event witnessed by the Dutch painter — a seventeenth-century operation for cataracts. Remembering an account of a miraculous cure for blindness, taken from the apocryphal bible, the Book of Tobit, the artist alters a detail in the narrative from which his painting takes its subject. In place of the magic concoction in the hands of the gold-turbaned physician of the tale, he substitutes a shining silver needle — thus conveying instantaneously the progress of medicine from biblical times to the seventeenth century and forecasting the miracles of the future.

# Broken Silence

Twenty-five years ago I lied
when they asked if I'd taken pictures. My photograph,
a silent open mouth — maybe that's the way
the neighbors felt when they swerved,
missed a collision, rolled the car into a ditch.
Over before they knew it; bruised faces, arms, little girl's
*what happened* from the back — they were OK.

In my photograph, the tilted horizon draws too little yellow
sky above red, six-foot banks of a bomb crater —
soldiers mill around — one sits forever on a duffel bag
holding his helmet, staring into it like he wants to vomit.
What you can't see is, inside
he's taped a picture of his wife.
Later he took a round through that helmet, never
looked at her again. Off to one side,

two ARVN soldiers in camouflage stand smoking.
One looks toward the high ground where trees
draw clean, black lines against yellow sky.
The other stares into a pit beside them, holds his rifle like a cane.
I like to think he's explaining some reality to the other.
Perhaps, how simple it would be if snipers were only smudges
on those lines. And all they did was reach out randomly
to tap our shoulders, faces, arms like you'd touch a sleepwalker.

I look up from my photo and out
the window where last month I watched the news
of the neighbors' accident spread. The bruised couple
sat on the porch — someone came to take the girl —
and all the while from the lawn or road,
one or two at a time, well-wishers called,
turned, shaking their heads, and walked away.

The man knelt down beside his wife,
smoothed her hair, touched her purple cheek.
His lips moved — she could barely nod.
In full view of the neighbors

he reached out his hand to cover hers.
But even if you look directly at my photograph
you still can't see the most important part. In the bottom of the pit,
beside the two smoking soldiers, an old woman,
a man and a four-year-old — suspected spies —
lie layered, one over the other. There was a scream
like a bird, but from a time before birds — a final shot —
then a great silence — my shutter clacked,
the only sound in the world.

RON CHARACH

# A Question of Vitamins

Lunch at The Mars,
squall jacket over my green surgical top.

One table over, this guy in a golf jacket
with a second man old enough to be his father,
a man with nothing in his grey eyes,
and shoulders so round
they looked stuffed,
or on leave from a hospital.
The young one tries to cheer him up.
"Dem docs, they don' like you takin' vitamins.
All they do is put you on these dangerous
drugs . . ."

And when he keeps on staring —

"True, it's not for everyone.
But, say a guy needs more B-7, or say, B-6,
then that's just what he *needs.*"

And when there's still no response,
he kneads the old man's arm.

"For some reason *your* brain needs more
of these vitamins.
I mean, they tell you,
'you don't *need* vitamins, your body makes its *own.*'

"Who are they kiddin'?
It's like sayin', Don't bother puttin' oil in your car,
just wait till you *run out.*
Like, Sandy knows this lady
who gave birth to a baby
who was short of B-vitamins. *Short.*
So how can they say you don't need extra,
that maybe *your patickular body*
don't need extra? So I axe 'em,
*Does* a body need vitamins,
Or *don't* it?"

He pushes on, a mix of hope and hate.

"Someday, what you're gonna see is *this*:
They're gonna charge people who smoke
and who *don't* take vitamins *more*
for their life insurance,
and people who don't smoke
and who *do* take vitamins, *less*."

I'm about to start in on my microwaved blintzes
when, sudden as a creak in a hinge,
the huge mountain of a father,
whose featureless back is all that stands
between me and mr. vitamins, says,

"Whadda you know?
You got a job?"

# Christmas, Belfast

*We have a Catholic mum and a Protestant mum here [in Belfast],*
*and they want us all to make friends for Christmas. I think they'll be*
*disappointed!*
— a nine-year-old Belfast girl whose parents dared "intermarry"


Waterford crystal smuggled from the Republic into Paisley's turf,
An excuse for the children to know beauty,
Stare into the infinity of a ball,
See, maybe, the light of God's birth
Still trying to hit our eyes,
Give us sight beyond our here.
"Ma, why did you sit with a Pape woman?"
"Ma, why did you smile at the Prod lady?"
But no matter the refrains,
The two sat in one church, another:
Visitors following the refractions through corridors of time,
Hoping the bleeding heart
(The one framed by the nuns)
Will stop altogether —
Become the new beat of an island's infant life.

They held hands, two mothers ready to toss
Paisley and the Pope to the wolves of Belfast,
Where blood is thicker than the mud,
The slime of the Irish Sea,
Where the traffic of hate, back and forth, began,
No matter His trip —
So important, the preachers say, to all of us.
"If we can come together on Christmas
Others can follow" — the old faith in leadership:
Come ye, follow me.
But soon a million roads,
Each got with bows and arrows, guns, planes:
The ascent of man it is called —
Our killing tools.

They spoke their dreams at noon,
The light of Norway passing them,

Trying for Greenland before a quick death.
If only they both could deliver on His birthday
A pair of celebrations, and all Ulster
Would take notice —
Leave bad words at the door,
The kitchen warm with their cooking.

ROBERT COLES

# The Goddam Street

I know her children,
have seen them getting ready
for what she calls
"the goddam street."
Each child has been held
and breast-fed in ways
well-nourished mothers might envy.
In the cold rat-infested flat
there is lively warmth
between mother and babies,
songs, smiles, sighs.
"I don't know how to do it,
how to keep my kids
from getting stained, ruined
I keep them close to me.
They can tell how much
I want for it to be good,
so, I hope they'll make it,
and I stop, say a prayer —
not expecting prayer to be
answered, not around here."

ROBERT COLES

# New Jersey Boys

*To W. C. W.*

You two gardeners,
Both you bards, Bruce and Bill,
The Boss and the Doc,
Who never wanted to skip
The heartbeat of home —
Stay there, your choice:
Claiming the spread below the Hudson.
No bridge or tunnel worked for you,
The local turf gave you plenty to do —
Soil to pick up with bare hands;
Bring sun to warm it up,
Let drafts of air turn it on,
See its excitement grow.
Let the twin tallest buildings in the world
Signal their dough to the torch-lady nearby;
Lots of folks who scare up the blinds in the morning
Are spared the hangout — the hangups — of the big shots.

You two gardeners and your trips to the city:
"The Lonely Street" was followed
Decades later by "Racing in the Streets."
Each of you made the trek:
So many hustles to see,
All the colors and sounds, the words and deals,
Cards to be dealt, decks stacked,
A throw of the dice daily:
Plain life and crying-shame deaths,
None of the Eros and Thanatos stuff
You hear in abstract elsewheres.
"Hey," you both pleaded,
"No starch in the shirts."

Both you gardeners raked:
Sweat all day and kiss
When you're lucky to find the lips.
No tax credits, just the tax itself, all the time,

Hoping for a break, a day off
Now and then, and the kids, they might do better,
Though it's always tough in Paterson,
And lots of times Nebraska is no picnic.

You guys, the gardener Walt's kin,
Whose beard we all know
(Its secrets keep a growth industry busy —
Leafing through his grass)
You two, from Ridge Road and E Street,
Each out to put it on the line, put them there:
Ordinary ones, whose lumps pollsters rush
To palpate only now and then.
You two are permanent guests,
Listening and showing your love in words, in notes
Two bards, Bruce and Bill,
The Boss and the Doc: America —
Love it or leave it to you both to know,
And give back to us, maybe our only chance.

JACK COULEHAN

# The Dynamizer and the Oscilloclast

*for Albert Abrams, an American quack*

1

Here is the machine, the dynamizer,
whose boxes, wires, and rheostats
reveal the hidden names of pain.
On the cot my assistant lies,
his scalp connected by a wire
to this, the measurement device
in which I place the drops of blood.
Then, I finger my assistant's skin
to find the place the patient's suffering.
He groans. The needle cries its name.

Poor distant people see my face
smiling from the back of magazines.
They send me shreds of paper
soaked in blood and tell their tales.
I am their savior, their last hope.
When I feed their stories, one by one,
here, into the mouth of this device,
my assistant moves, the needle turns.
YES! I write them. Come. Come soon.
For I have named your suffering.

2

One more rheostat, another gauge.
At night in my basement shop
I work on the oscilloclast,
a new machine that oscillates disease,
restores the harmony of health.
In my mind's ear the oscilloclast
already sings. There! Can you hear
those songs, those streams, those crickets?

When I rush to fit their frequencies
to my machine, the music disappears.

The sick are selling their farms in Kansas.
They are buying their tickets in Georgia.
They are putting their houses in order.
My letters told them, Come! Come soon!
What could I do but give them hope?
They're here. The sick are pounding at my door.
I must finish the oscilloclast tonight!
One more rheostat, a final gauge,
and then, my friends, the sick, come in.

# Lovesickness: A Medieval Text

As real as melancholy, baldness, headache,
or scalp lice. As real as Christ's love for his bride
the Church. As real as an imbalance of bile
in the brain's ventricles, tumbling the lover
ever forward with sad sighs and hidden thoughts.
As real as the surge of moist heat that collects
in the second ventricle and thus creates
in the first, a cold, dry atmosphere — stunned sense.
As real as a parched mouth, an edematous tongue,
a bitterness in the throat, as though the patient
had eaten unripe plums. As real as rapture,
but as pale in complexion as spent humor.

Cures include travel, which diminishes languor
and permits the beloved's image to lessen
in potency. The deep induction of sleep
by medicinal herbs, which wipe clean the slate.
Wine, conversation, and the reading of books,
which serve as cathartics, purging the patient's
obsessions. Litigation, or bringing a suit,
may also be helpful, by putting an edge
on the mind's collapse. In the most serious
cases, all these remedies are likely to fail —
in extremis, prescribe sexual relations,
following which a cure will usually occur.

RICHARD DONZE

# Vermont Has a High Suicide Rate

at least that's
what Paul says
and he

should know,
he's a doctor
there, near Burlington

who supplements his income
with farming and
maple sugaring, and

makes the kind
of money in
twelve months that

a megalopolitan madman
might go through
in two, and lives

more simply than simple,
can go
to work with

muddy boots, has
a fine beard,
and is happy.

Why, I ask
in a place
that means green

mountain, where what
look like clouds
actually are,

and the land
is the way,
not in the

way, of life
are the people
killing themselves?

It's the winters,
Paul says,
people can get

crazy when it's
so cold
so long.

THOMAS DORSETT

# The Survivor

*Dresden, 1945 / Baltimore, 1995*

She saw on her home street
a host of Judgment soldiers
plunder everything,
crack shock troops of total war,
each a six-foot flame.

"Momma, that was many years ago."
It's as if she hears angels
confined to the head of a match
scream in pain as it ignites: among them
her parents and their youngest child.

Her family fled to the cellar:
she ran outside, terrorized
by an army of flames,
running without looking back
until she reached Maryland.

She never talked about it
until one day in her old age
the low drone of a jet became
a flock of bombers: she ran outside,
fleeing the heat of her stove.

"Our house is on fire, our house is on fire . . ."
Come, this will put the fire out,
I tell her; a Sisyphus task,
trying to put out the fires of hell
with spoonfuls of nursing-home Jell-O.

# The Pain

From some unsought somewhere
in the raucous transactions
of my life, the pain has scraped
acquaintance, selecting its
spot, nestling in the backroom,
down in the basement of my bones.

Mostly it's unobtrusive, keeps
out of my bedroom and my parlor.
But I'll still sense it out there,
perched on my hot back stoop in wait.
So when company comes I slip it a
drug for dinner, and for a time

there's not a peek from it. And I
start to dare scarcely to hope
it's at last skulked out by a
back exit from my place, seeking
more congenial rooms. Then over
the dawn birdcall I'll wake to

its dull knock on the dark
door and, if I dare disregard it,
flinch to insistent thrump of
knuckles on my ceiling, clunk upon
my skull. Then I'll know to lay
its place again at table.

# Number Our Days

*So teach us to number our days,*
*that we may get us a heart of wisdom.*
— Psalm 90

Names.
She and my uncles looked for names.
Who survived, who didn't survive.
Who was there, who wasn't there?
Which ghetto, which *platz*, which platform,
which side-track, which car, which camp,
which barrack, which bunk . . .

How could you leave them behind?
Even when they said,
"We're too old to run,
take the baby and save your life."
Maybe you don't think about it.
Maybe you don't think,
your heart too fast for your breath,
your tongue thick, the words won't come . . .

24 hours, the gestapo officer said,
24 hours, or you're *all* done.

\*

She took the train going west,
my blonde head suckling her breast,
her fingers touching the crucifix.
Too scared, too brave to look up, she saw
only the boots, heard only their heels salute.

\*

For years after,
she vomited a lot, soundless like a dog,
coming back to the table smelling a bit, wiping her lips.
It became easier not to eat.

How well-behaved I had to be for her,
how proud she was of her doctor son,
as I rubbed and kissed arthritic hands.
But then her rage laid pincers on my tongue.

*

The gas oven we had
was a Kelvinator.
I was at home when she put in her head.
Later she said, "Don't tell your father."
After that I hoped each day to come home from school
and find her dead.

*

170, 152, 127,
her weight dropped like a stone, 98,
when it went under 80
she hid the scale —
and nothing I did
could avert its final decree.

When the doctors proposed dialysis
my father moaned, unable to speak,
and three uncles howled at *me* —
"Save her life! Save her life!"

As if it were now mine to decide
on that ugly night:
dialyzed mothers to the left,
dead mothers to the right.

# Prediction

The world might end in crispness
like a smack on the bottom at birth.
A division of skin or fascia at autopsy.
The closing doors, the departure
of planes. Endings without confetti.
An unpeddled note on a harpsichord.

I think the world will end in Houston.
Mold, an extrusion of hyphae on formica.
Accretion of residues and gels. As a mollusk.
Even aluminum will rust. Small animals
will decompose, ferns will grow, pterodactyls
will fly, thick as the day the world began.

# Voyeur

A man watches a woman disrobe in a window,
Which is not unusual, except each has walked
On this earth for almost eighty years
To arrive at such epiphany. Confusing grief
With desire, he believes in the absolute
Loneliness of the dark, in liberation
Snap by snap from the chrysalis
Of a dress, pretends that this is his dead wife
Fluttering long ago in the footlights of a dive
In New Orleans to bear up their struggling lives.
How that crowd of red and sweaty faces
Envied him, he thinks amid the roses.
As if peering from shadows into the undrawn shades
Of his own life, he catches a bright glimpse
Through the sheer surface of longing —
As close as we come to some modest human beauty,
The body as epitome of the soul.
Because guilt and fear intertwine,
He keeps his visions to himself until one night
After bourbon, when his son wants to know
If he still misses his wife, the man leads him
Among trees and stars to the precarious edge
Of his neighbor's world to watch her unveil
For her bath at ten, hoping to redeem
One passion or another. When the son, who prefers
Principles to fantasy, storms off,
The man starts to wonder if he ever loved his wife.
Maybe she was nothing all those years
But the dim flash of thighs or quiver of buttocks.
It's you I love, he says to the wedding portrait
In its gold-edged pane above the fireplace.
It's you I know, he says to Polaroids
Of her cocooned in a hospital bed for the next life.
Then one evening the woman sees him,
And lets curtains fall as on a small stage.
But because to walk naked before someone

Is to enter an intimate unknown, she too hears
Raucous music from her past, finds herself
Flushed and a little less alone;
And because the bleakest salvation
Still saves, she imagines herself loved,
Less profane, perhaps, but well consumed, the flesh
Impervious to all dishonors but one.

DAVID MOOLTEN

# Brandy Station, Virginia

A few miles from here, they've unearthed
A young Confederate soldier.
The historians already know which night
He died, how far his elite unit tramped
Along the Rappahannock River
Through a limbo of gunsmoke, the burnt straw
And brimstone of dueling artillery,
The claiming of both sides. They know
That right there on the Fredricksburg-
Winchester Road, survivors pulled pews
Out of the St. James Episcopal Church,
That having no time and "meaning no sacrilege"
The men carpentered crudely, houses
For the dead from the house of God.
They can describe, with painstaking precision,
The rifle pits, the rations and harnesses,
The grade of bullets, the fire of logs
And fence rails like a vigil light.
Even I can reconstruct the encircling
Dark wood, and crickets in the keen
Of life, how the hearts of the living
Eulogize with shrill fear and gratitude,
With perseveration: *not me, not me, not me.*
It was a week before the second Bull Run.
The old brick church itself would fall later,
As churches fall in such a forest
Like a tree that makes no sound, and in more
Than a century they'd marvel over his skeleton,
The buttons from his coat, his pipe;
And the wood, perhaps they'd wonder
If it was ever holy or just wood,
Like the tall planks Christ was laid on.

DAVID MOOLTEN

# Madame Butterfly

When a half-crazed woman stepped aboard
Our trolleycar one night screaming
At someone no longer there who can say
What it was that made me understand
That I was her, that all of us were?
Perhaps it was the high pitch of her convictions
That made me think of Butterfly raising her voice
From that hillside above the calm waves
Which drew her lover's ship like all that's bottomless
And wrenching and always smoothed with reason
Or faith into the acceptable: more tuneful
Perhaps, but deranged with the same earnest grief.
Who can say a change of seats or a glance
Aimed skillfully aside was not just collusion
To be insanely silent in the face
Of unbearable tragedy we call everyday life?
All of us must be screaming as we lose
What we learn too late was ours, a diva
Somewhere inside to which we rarely listen.
The point is: no one sang. No one even spoke.
Dragged by that streetcar a little further
Towards the same place, we just turned
From each other harder, seeing mostly our own
Reflections and not the dark tenements, the defunct
Deus ex machina of a water tower like props
For a scene because a scene is what one tries
So politely to avoid. It was as if our eyes
Had become accustomed to epiphany while between us
The chance was forever lost in those few
Hushed moments. Who can say why we prefer
The role of the duty-bound, why we choose
Decorum over passion until we can't
Tell the difference? The only butterfly that night
Was a scream. It passed over us like foreign words.
It vanished behind our silence like a song
A man never turns to hear from the firm land

Where he's needed while the deep water
Of his fate tugs with no more than its motion
Onwards. How could we know that this
Was the music of our lives?

# The Truck

I was coming back from
wherever I'd been when
I saw the truck and
the sign on the back repeated
on the side to be certain
you knew it was no mistake

PROGRESS CASKETS

ARTHUR ILLINOIS

Now folks have different
thoughts it's true about
death but in general it's
not like any race for
example you ever ran
everyone wanting to come in

last and all    And I admit
a business has to have a good
name    No one knows better
than I the value of a good
name    A name is what sells
the product in the first

and in the final place
All this time the Interstate
was leading me into Atlanta
and I was following the sign
and the truck was heavier
climbing the hill than

going down which is as
it should be    What I really
wanted to see was the driver
up close maybe talk to him
find out his usual run
so I could keep off it

Not that I'm superstitious    It's just
the way I was raised    A casket
may be Progress up in Arthur
but it's thought of
down here
as a setback.

# Getting to Sleep in New Jersey

Not twenty miles from where I work,
William Williams wrote after dark,

after the last baby was caught,
knowing that what he really ought

to do was sleep. Rutherford slept,
while all night William Williams kept

scratching at his prescription pad,
dissecting the good lines from the bad.

He tested the general question whether
feet or butt or head-first ever

determines as well the length of labor
of a poem. His work is over:

bones and guts and red wheelbarrows;
the loneliness and all the errors

a heart can make the other end
of a stethoscope. Outside, the wind

corners the house with a long crow.
Silently, his contagious snow

covers the banks of the Passaic River,
where he walked once, full of fever,

tracking his solitary way
back to his office and the white day,

a peculiar kind of bright-eyed bird,
hungry for morning and the perfect word.

# Will Campbell Displays His Craniotribe

They said I had to have it. It was an instrument
in those days as fundamental as forceps, as much
a part of country practice as the witches' touch,
pink eye, my healing hands, or the black bag.

It's meant more to impress than to be used.
The vets have something like it for birthing calves
dead or too big to deliver except in halves.
The children *ooh* when I turn it loose.

I never use it, but it's like a badge, a token
of my occupation. Sometimes I still go out
to the home if it's a multip I know. And I'll put
this thing down on the kitchen table and snap it open,
just joking, of course, and tell the father what
it's for. That gets him out of the room and the woman
always laughs, appreciating my act, even though
she's about to undergo something she'd rather not.

It's for the occasional monster, you see,
sideshow oddities, conjoined twins, hydrocephalus.
But I turned out to be only a country doctor, a woolhat
like my patients. How was I to know
I'd never run across monsters in a lifetime,
I who was chosen by mischance for this work
and delivered two thousand normals playing stork
in the thirty-bed hospital here at Humble Pie?

# Insulin Receptor

*Musings on a technical paper*

So elegant, so simple, yet thought
will not advance to speech until this string
of acids taps a passerby, which caught
makes everything

happen. The energy for laugh
or sprinter's spurt or belly-dancer's slink
comes from the kinase insulin tips off
as it is firmly clinched.

Movement and words are simple things
made possible by dropping phosphate ions.
The carbon chains that sweep the eagle's wings
empower science

and art alike. But know that if,
in the complex of mutually dependent pieces
a lysine in the trap is moved a bit,
everything ceases.

That's all it takes to keep the most big-hearted
mammal from activating tyrosyls.
Sometimes I wonder how we ever started
when an almost-nothing kills.

# Damien

Hardly a day goes by I don't think of him
on Molokai: that first night

sleeping outside under a pandanus tree,
awakened by screams

and hideous faces floating
in the white gauze of moonlight.

That first day in sunlight, so much
glittering pain. I see him brushing back

a tendril of hair sweated to a brown face,
saying the words that bring hope.

I see him anointing feet
covered with pustules, burying a cadaver

behind a picket fence so the pigs
can't get it. His was a priesthood of worms

and rotting flesh. And sixteen years
later when they buried him

under the same pandanus tree,
the plot contained two thousand graves.

Most of all I see the picture of him
taken weeks before his death.

It shows a joke of a man
posed in a dirty black robe, a battered

priest-hat, its broad brim
tied up with strings, and wire spectacles.

The face is as ruined
as an old boxer's face: cauliflower

ears, flattened nose, lumpy cheeks.
It's the face of a thick

peasant from Tremeloo, Belgium,
not fit to hold high office in his own

church. It's the face
of a leper. And that picture burns itself

into the retina
like ragged lightning in the night sky.

# The Miracle

The old man, seated, his boiled turnip eyes
   turned toward the window, groans like a broken windmill
     touched by the wind,
as Dr. Job Janszoon van Meekren inserts a silver needle
   carefully into one eye and begins to tease aside the tiny glob
     of dirty egg-white, the cataract.

In a pot on the window sill, a carnage
of pink and red tulips: the first thing the old man will see.

Amsterdam, 1636.

After witnessing this operation, Rembrandt
   stumbles out, shaken
     into the swirling dust of *Sint Antoniesbreestraat*
and begins running, oblivious to the dogs, the beggars, two men
     butchering an ox in a stall, the old woman
   frying pancakes on the corner.

"If only my father
were still alive," he shouts. "His blindness
   could be cured!" Already
     in the black lake of his mind, three trembling moons
are coalescing. He is remembering a miracle
     in the apocryphal bible, The Book
   of Tobit, about how a son magically heals his father's blindness
     with the help of an angel.

Breathless, at home, he begins.
   On a black canvas, the trembling moons
     become the bleached white faces of
   the angel Raphael, brow furrowed, wings spread wide; the old man
Tobit, seated, turned toward the window, with a long beard; and, leaning
   over, concentrating, with a small mustache, a gold
     turban on his head, the son Tobias.

And through the open window comes
     the scalding light, sweet as grace, shining
   on Tobias's hand, holding not

a bowl of the magic gall from a disemboweled fish, as the biblical story
    tells it,
but a silver needle, poised
above the blind eye.

# Permissions

Louis M. Abbey. "Broken Silence," *Seattle Review*, 1997.

Dannie Abse. "The Doctor," "Lunch and Afterwards," "The Stethoscope," "Millie's Date," "Pathology of Colours," "X-Ray," "In the Theatre," and "Carnal Knowledge" reprinted with permission of the Peters Fraser and Dunlop Group Limited on behalf of *White Coat, Purple Coat: Collected Poems*, Persea Books, 1991; "The Origin of Music" reprinted with permission of the Peters Fraser and Dunlop Group Limited on behalf of *Remembrance of Crimes Past*, Persea Books, 1993.

Rafael Campo. "El Curandero" and "Towards Curing A I D S " reprinted with permission from the publisher of *The Other Man Was Me* (Houston: University of Houston, Arte Público Press, 1994). "What the Body Told," "Her Final Show," and "S. W." from *What the Body Told*, © 1996, Duke University Press. Reprinted with permission.

Ron Charach. "The Evidence on Film," *Dalhousie Review* (Spring 1979), and "A Question of Vitamins," *New England Journal of Medicine* (1989). "Labour and Delivery" appeared in *The Naked Physician*, edited by Ron Charach, © 1990. Reprinted by permission of Quarry Press, Kingston, Ontario "MRI," *Past Wildflowers*, by Ron Charach, 1997. Reprinted by permission of Quarry Press.

Robert Coles. "The Goddam Street" from *A Festering Sweetness: Poems of American People*, by Robert Coles, © 1978. Reprinted with permission of the University of Pittsburgh Press. "Christmas, Belfast," "New Jersey Boys," and "On Dutch's Death" from *Rumors of Separate Worlds*, by Robert Coles, © 1989. Reprinted by permission of the University of Iowa Press.

Jack Coulehan. "I'm Gonna Slap Those Doctors" and "Anatomy Lesson" from *The Knitted Glove*, Nightshade Press, 1991; "The Man with a Hole in His Face," "The Dynamizer and the Oscilloclast," and "The Rule of Thirds" from *First Photographs of Heaven*, Nightshade Press, 1994. The following poems first appeared in the *Journal of the American Medical Association*: "D-Day, 1994" (1995), "The Azalea Poem" (1997), and "Lovesickness: A Medieval Text" (1997), © 1995 and 1997, American Medical Association. Reprinted with permission.

Richard Donze. "Vermont Has a High Suicide Rate," *Annals of Internal Medicine*, 1986.

Thomas Dorsett. "The Survivor," *Dance Fire Dance* (Baltimore: Icarus Books, 1993).

Kirsten Emmott. "Who Looks after Your Kids?" from *How Do You Feel?* (Victoria, B.C.: Sono Nis Press, 1992).

D. A. Feinfeld. "Carmelita" and "The Wound Man" from *What Do Numbers Dream Of?* University Editions, 1997.

James L. Foy. "Autopsy" from *Medical Heritage*, 1986.

Arthur Ginsberg. "The Chief of Medicine" from *Journal of the American Medical*

*Association*, May 1, 1996, ©1996, American Medical Association. Reprinted with permission.

John Graham-Pole. "Venipuncture," *Annals of Internal Medicine*, 1994; "The Pain," *Archives of Family Medicine*, 1994; "Leaving Mother, 1954," *APPA Newsletter*, Spring 1997.

Grace Herman. "The Clinic," *Set Against Darkness*, National Council of Jewish Women, New York, 1992.

Eugene Hirsch. "Two Suffering Men," *Journal of Medical Humanities*, 1992.

Norbert Hirschhorn. "Number Our Days," *Prairie Schooner*.

Alice Jones. "Tap," *Ploughshares*, Winter 1996–97. "Anorexia" and "Communal Living" from *The Knot* by Alice Jones, © 1992. Reprinted with permission of Alice James Books, Cambridge, Mass.

Michael Lieberman. "Regret," "Prediction," "Los Olivos," and "On the Anniversary of My Father's Death" from *A History of the Sweetness of the World* by Michael Lieberman, © 1995. Reprinted with permission of Texas Review Press.

David Moolten. "Madame Butterfly," *North American Review* Nov.–Dec. 1995. "Bio 7," "Brandy Station, Virginia," "Motorcycle Ward," and "Voyeur" from *Plums and Ashes* by David Moolten, © 1994. Reprinted with permission of Northeastern University Press.

Jon Mukand. "Lullaby" and "First Payment" appeared in *Sutured Words: Contemporary Poetry about Medicine*, edited by Jon Mukand, 1987. "Lullaby" reprinted in *Articulations: The Body and Illness in Poetry*, edited by Jon Mukand. Reprinted with permission of the University of Iowa Press.

Michael O'Reilly. "potter," *The Lancet*, 1996. "abused child," *Journal of Family Practice*, 1994. Reprinted by permission of Appleton and Lange, Inc. "a house call to a man with parkinson's disease" and "a small girl brings an injured bird into the surgery," *Perspectives in Biology and Medicine*, Winter 1992.

Frederic W. Platt. "Coincidentally," *Fetishes: A Literary Journal of the University of Colorado Health Science Center*, 1997.

Elspeth Cameron Ritchie. "Electroconvulsive Therapy" (an earlier version), *Convulsive Therapy*, 1993.

Vernon Rowe. "MRI of a Poet's Brain," "Youth," and "Time Heals All Wounds — But One" from *Sea Creatures and Other Poems*, Whirlybird Press, 1995.

Audrey Shafer. "Monday Morning," *Annals of Internal Medicine*, 1992, anthologized in *On Being a Doctor*, ed. Michael A. LaCombe, American College of Physicians, 1995. "Gurney Tears," *Journal of Medical Humanities*, 1995.

John Stone. "Talking to the Family" and "Getting to Sleep in New Jersey" from *The Smell of Matches*, 1976; "He Makes a House Call" and "The Truck" from *In All This Rain*, 1980; "Rosemary," "Confabulation," "The Bass," and "*Gaudeamus Igitur*: A Valediction," *Renaming the Street*, 1985. Reprinted with permission of Louisiana State University Press.

Marc J. Straus. "Luck," "The Log of Pi," "Scarlet Crown," "What I Heard on the Radio Today," and "Neuroanatomy Summer" from *One Word* by Marc J.

# Contributors

LOUIS M. ABBEY is an oral and maxillofacial pathologist and professor of pathology at Virginia Commonwealth University/Medical College of Virginia. He is a Vietnam veteran, and his poetry has appeared in national literary magazines. He lives and writes in Richmond, Virginia.

DANNIE ABSE is a practicing physician and one of Great Britain's foremost poets. He is the author of nine books of poetry, several plays, three novels, and two autobiographical works. *White Coat, Purple Coat: Collected Poems* was published in the United States in 1993.

ANGELA BELLI is professor of English at St. John's University in New York. She has had an enduring interest in comparative and interdisciplinary studies. Her first book, *Ancient Greek Myths and Modern Drama: A Study in Continuity*, was published by New York University Press. She has contributed many articles, book chapters, and reviews to literary and medical publications. She is a frequent participant in the meetings of professional organizations devoted to the study of literature and to the advancement of the medical humanities and was recently elected to the board of directors of the New York College English Association.

RAFAEL CAMPO teaches and practices general internal medicine at Harvard Medical School and Beth Israel Deaconess Medical Center in Boston. He is the author of *The Other Man Was Me* (1994), which won the 1993 National Poetry Series Award; *What the Body Told* (1996), which won a Lambda Literary Award for Poetry; and *The Poetry of Healing: A Doctor's Education in Empathy, Identity, and Desire* (1996), a collection of essays.

RON CHARACH born in Winnipeg, now practices psychiatry in Toronto. He is the author of three poetry collections, including *The Big Life Painting* (1987), *Someone Else's Memoirs* (1994), and *Past Wildflowers* (1997). In 1990 he edited the anthology *The Naked Physician: Poems about the Lives of Patients and Doctors*.

ROBERT COLES is professor of psychiatry and medical humanities at Harvard University. He has devoted his career to studying the inner lives of children all over the world and is the author of the seminal *Children of Crisis* series, for which he won a Pulitzer Prize. Among his many other books are biographies of Simone Weil, Dorothy Day, and Anna Freud; *The Call of Stories: Teaching and the Moral Imagination* (1989); and the recent best-selling *The Moral Intelligence of Children* (1996). His books of poetry include *A Festering Sweetness* (1978) and *Rumors of Separate Worlds* (1989).

JACK COULEHAN is professor of medicine and preventive medicine at the State University of New York at Stony Brook and the director of Stony Brook's Institute for Medicine in Contemporary Society. He practices general internal medicine and teaches physician-patient communication as well as medical humanities. His latest book is *The Medical Interview: Mastering Skills for*

*Clinical Practice* (1997). His two collections of poetry are *The Knitted Glove* (1991) and *First Photographs of Heaven* (1994).

RICHARD DONZE is a physician-poet whose work has appeared frequently in *JAMA* and other publications. Board-certified in family practice and preventive medicine, Donze currently practices occupational medicine in West Chester. His first book, *Dinner Music*, is due out in 1998.

THOMAS DORSETT is a pediatrician with the Johns Hopkins Medical Corporation. His books include a poetry collection, *Dance Fire Dance* (1994), a German translation of Jim Wayne Miller's *Copperhead Crane (Der Schlangenstock*, 1995), and *Beyond These Shores* (1996), a translation of recently discovered poems and the diary of a young Jewish woman who wrote in Nazi Germany from 1934 until 1939.

ERIC DYER, a pulmonary specialist, began writing poetry seriously during his years of medical education at Vanderbilt and Yale. He was born in rural Illinois; he and his wife, Cheryl, now live in Nashville. In addition to pursuing his medical, literary, and other interests, Dyer currently is restoring an antique Farmall tractor similar to ones owned by his father and grandfather.

KIRSTEN EMMOTT was born in Edmonton, Alberta. She is the mother of two children and lives in Comox, B.C., where she practices as a family doctor. Her most recent book is *How Do You Feel?* (1992).

D. A. FEINFELD is codirector of the nephrology service at Nassau County Medical Center in New York and associate professor of clinical medicine at the State University of New York at Stony Brook. His first collection of poetry, *What Do Numbers Dream Of?* appeared in 1997.

JAMES L. FOY is a retired academic physician living in Maryland after earlier careers as a U.S. Navy flight surgeon and psychiatrist on the faculty of Georgetown University. Poetry has been a collateral occupation and close companion since his days as a medical student.

ARTHUR GINSBERG practices neurology in Seattle. His first book of poetry, *Walking the Panther*, was published in 1984. His poetry has frequently appeared in medical and literary journals, and he is a past winner of "Bumbershoot."

JOHN GRAHAM-POLE is professor of pediatrics and a pediatric oncologist at the University of Florida School of Medicine. He is the codirector of both the Arts in Medicine Program and the Holistic Health Group at the University of Florida Health Sciences Center, where he also performs as an improvisational actor and clown. His poems have appeared in many medical periodicals.

GRACE HERMAN is a retired physician who has written poetry for more than thirty-five years. Her poems have appeared in the *Minnesota Review, Poetry Review of the Poetry Society of America, Literature and Medicine, Embers*, and *Poetalk*, among other magazines, and were collected in *Set Against Darkness* (1992).

EUGENE HIRSCH is a retired cardiologist and geriatrician who lives in Pittsburgh. He taught for many years at Case Western Reserve School of Medicine and more recently at the University of Tennessee. His poems have appeared in many journals, and several were recently anthologized in *The Tyranny of the Normal* (1996).

NORBERT HIRSCHHORN is the director of the Division of Family Health, Minnesota Department of Health. He has an MFA in poetry from Vermont College. His chapbook of poems, *Renewal Soup*, was published in 1996 by Slow Dancer Press.

ALICE JONES is a psychiatrist and psychoanalysist who practices in Oakland. She is the author of *The Knot* (1992), winner of the Beatrice Hawley Award, and of a chapbook, *Anatomy* (1997). One of her poems appeared in *Best American Poetry of 1994*.

MICHAEL LIEBERMAN is a research physician who chairs the Department of Pathology at Baylor University College of Medicine in Houston. He is the author of *Praising with My Body* (1992), *A History of the Sweetness of the World*, which won the Texas Review's Breakthrough Contest for new poets in 1995, and *Goldin at Elmhurst* (1998).

DAVID MOOLTEN was born in Boston in 1961. He currently resides in Philadelphia, where he works as a pathologist. His poems have appeared in numerous periodicals, including the *Georgia Review*, *Poetry*, *North American Review*, *Southern Review*, and *Sewanee Review*. His first book, *Plums and Ashes*, was awarded the Samuel French Morse Poetry Prize in 1994.

JON MUKAND practices physical medicine and rehabilitation in Providence, Rhode Island, and has completed a Ph.D. in literature at Brown University. In addition to publishing numerous poems, he is the editor of *Articulations: The Body and Illness in Poetry* (1995) and *Vital Lines: Contemporary Fiction about Medicine* (1990).

MICHAEL O'REILLY was a young general practitioner in Ireland. His poems have been widely published in British and American medical journals. Michael died at his home in Dundalk, County Louth, in March 1988.

EDMUND D. PELLEGRINO is currently John Carroll Professor of Medicine and Medical Ethics at the Center for Clinical Bioethics, Georgetown University. He was the founding dean of the Medical School at the State University of New York at Stony Brook. His earlier positions include chancellor of the University of Tennessee, president of the Yale–New Haven Medical Center, and president of the Catholic University of America. He is the author or editor of twelve books, including *Humanism and the Physician* (1979) and (with David Thomasma) *The Virtues in Medical Practice* (1993).

FREDERIC W. PLATT practices internal medicine in Denver. He has written extensively on medical interviewing and the physician-patient relationship, including two books, *Conversation Failure* (1992) and *Conversation Repair* (1995). He is also a poet.

ELSPETH CAMERON RITCHIE is chief of inpatient psychiatry at Walter Reed Health Care Systems. She has served in the Army for twelve years and has been stationed in Washington, D.C., Korea, and Somalia. She lives in Maryland with her husband, daughter Jessie, and four cats. Her poetry has been published in a variety of medical and military journals and anthologies.

159

VERNON ROWE is in the private practice of neurology in Kansas City, where he uses a small helicopter to visit clinics in surrounding rural communities. *Sea Creatures*, his first book of poems, was published in 1995.

AUDREY SHAFER is an assistant professor of anesthesiology at Stanford University School of Medicine and staff anesthesiologist at the Palo Alto Veterans Affairs Health Care System. She teaches literature and medicine to medical and undergraduate students and has published poetry in medical and literary journals.

JOHN STONE, a cardiologist, is professor of medicine and associate dean for admissions at Emory University School of Medicine. His three books of poetry are *The Smell of Matches* (1976), *In All This Rain* (1980), and *Renaming the Streets* (1985). He is also the author of *In the Country of Hearts* (1993), a book of essays and stories, and is coeditor, with Richard Reynolds, of the anthology *On Doctoring* (1995).

MARC J. STRAUS, formerly chief of oncology at New York Medical College, practices medical oncology in White Plains, N.Y. *One Word*, his first collection of poetry, was published in 1994; and a chapbook, *Scarlet Crown*, appeared the same year. His newest collection is *Not God* (1998). His poems have appeared in *TriQuarterly*, *Ploughshares*, *Kenyon Review*, *Virginia Quarterly*, *Poetry East*, and elsewhere. In 1993 he was a Yaddo fellow.

PAULA TATARUNIS, an internist, was born in 1952 and lives and works near Boston. Her work has appeared in such journals as *Cream City Review*, *Literary Review*, *Exquisite Corpse*, *Formalist*, *Nedge*, *JAMA*, and *Massachusetts Review*. She received a Massachusetts Artists Foundation Fellowship in Poetry in 1987.

H. J. VAN PEENEN is a retired pathologist who lives in Salem, Oregon. His stories and poems have appeared in numerous periodicals. He published a collection of his light verse under the pseudonym of Morton Pollycove, M.D. (*The Literature*, 1992).

JOHN WRIGHT is clinical professor emeritus at the University of Washington. He practiced internal medicine and endocrinology in Seattle from 1964 to 1994, during which time he held the positions of director of education and medical director at the Swedish Medical Center. His poems and short stories have appeared in *JAMA*, *Annals of Internal Medicine*, *Journal of Family Practice*, and *Bulletin of the King County Medical Society*.

GEORGE YOUNG practices internal medicine and rheumatology at the Boulder Medical Center in Boulder, Colorado. He has been widely published in literary magazines. His first full-length collection of poems, *Spinoza's Mouse* (1996), won the 1996 Washington Prize in Poetry.